Peter
Enjoy the journey "...m"
& call me with q'
Cary
Oct 2019.

Overcoming Your NegotiaPhobia

Negotiating Your Way Through Life

by

Larry Waldman, PhD, ABPP
Cary Silverstein, MBA

Books That Work

Scottsdale, Arizona

Overcoming Your NegotiaPhobia: Negotiating Your Way Through Life
by Larry Waldman, PhD, ABPP, and Cary Silverstein, MBA

Printed in the United States of America
Published 2016
First Edition

20 19 18 17 16   1 2 3 4 5

ISBN-13: 978-1537768809

Library of Congress Control Number: 2016916028
CreateSpace Independent Publishing Platform, North Charleston, SC

Editor: Carolyn Kott Washburne
Designer and Typographer: Kate Hawley
Production Coordinator: Susan Pittelman

Published by

Books That Work

10071 East Turquoise Ave, Scottsdale, AZ 85258
BooksThatWorkAZ@aol.com

Dedicated to our wives Nan and Susie
for their patience as we took this literary journey.

Acknowledgments

Prior to publishing this book, we reached out to our friends, relatives, and topic experts to preview chapters and to provide real-life examples for discussion. We thank them for taking the time to assist us with "making it real" for our readers.

Thank you to Dr. Dennis Butler, PhD, a longtime friend and colleague, who offered examples for the topic of negotiating with your physician. To Attorney Gregg Herman, a fellow Rotarian and friend, who was kind enough to help with the chapters on marriage and divorce: your counsel was appreciated. To Mrs. Cese Holland for her expertise as an experienced realtor: thank you for consulting on the real estate section. To Rabbi Marc Berkson of Congregation Emanu-El B'ne Jeshurun, a dear friend and spiritual advisor: we thank you for your guidance and insights on the chapter on marriage.

A special thank you to Attorney Mark Goldstein for his insights and comments on the section on family business. Thank you to Christine Specht, president of Cousins Subs, for her time and input into the family business section. Her comments were very valuable. We are especially appreciative of Dr. Yasmin Davidds, PsyD, for her review of the chapter "Understanding Gender and Cultural Differences" and for generously sharing the content of her new book *Your Own Terms: A Women's Guide to Taking Charge of Any Negotiation*.

For their editing talents and their many editorial suggestions, we thank Dr. Breyne Moskowitz, PhD, and Clifton Batchelor of WorldPress Consulting and Internet Marketing. We also thank Jon Schnur, executive chairman of America Achieves, for his suggestions and comments.

Additional thanks go to the professionals, Carolyn Kott Washburne, Kate Hawley, and Susan Pittelman, who polished up our prose, created the book design, and coordinated the production of *Overcoming Your NegotiaPhobia*.

To our loving wives Susie Silverstein and Nan Waldman for giving their personal time and supplying their moral support, so we could write this book: we love you and thank you for your patience and understanding.

Finally, to our children Josh, Chad, Lesley, and Bradley: thank you for providing us with the many "real-life" examples from your childhood and colorful teenage years. We look forward to many future negotiations with you, our grandchildren, and their children.

Table of Contents

Introduction
Welcome to the World of Negotiation

Samantha, a young associate in a law firm, is having her first performance appraisal with her immediate supervisor and the managing attorney. Samantha does not agree with their ratings on her performance, which supports an average salary increase of two percent. She believes her performance was above average to excellent and that she deserves a four percent increase. The problem is that she is afraid to speak up and challenge their perceptions. She is concerned about "rocking the boat" by stating her case. Samantha begrudgingly accepts the average salary increase.

Diagnosis: "negotiaphobia"—the fear of negotiating anything. Negotiaphobia has raised its ugly head, and Samantha feels a high level of discomfort in a situation that involves an exchange of information. She needed to be better able to defend her position. The cure for her would have been to be better prepared with information and data that supported her version of how she performed.

Negotiaphobia is neither new nor uncommon, and many individuals suffer from this condition. This topic was first addressed in 2010 in *The One Minute Manager* by Don Hutson and George Lucas. They defined "negotiaphobia" as a widely present fear of negotiating based on a desire to avoid conflict. No one is comfortable in a situation that involves conflict; in fact, many people see themselves as "conflict adverse." They will do

1

anything to avoid a conflict with another individual, especially someone they have a relationship with, love, or admire.

As we move along life's journey, we encounter many decisions, challenges, and problems that require the use of strong communication and negotiation skills. Our personalities play a major role in how we negotiate, especially when we aren't aware of own tendencies; those tendencies are learned behaviors, honed by experience and sharpened by acquired knowledge.

As experienced social scientists, our goals are to provide you, the reader, with insights and strategies that will assist you in dealing with these challenging, conflict-ridden situations. In addition, our goal is to lessen your fear of negotiating anything, thus reducing your level of negotiaphobia.

Interacting with the members of your family can involve high levels of emotion and can be more difficult than dealing with people outside of the family unit. Yet dealing with toxic friends, bosses, and strangers can also provoke high levels of negotiaphobia. This is why you need to acquire the specific negotiation skills for the particular discussion or situation being encountered—to help you increase the potential for success in any negotiation you pursue.

In *Overcoming Your NegotiaPhobia,* we follow a number of hypothetical partners and situations, using real-life examples, and discuss how to prepare for, initiate, and successfully complete a sensitive negotiation affecting family members, including parents, children, and spouses. Some of the topics to be covered include deciding on when (or whether) to get married, buying a home, whether and when to have children, and how to discipline your children. In addition, we address buying/selling a car, or just dealing with a major purchase. Business transactions that you might encounter on a daily basis are also discussed. Different types of conflict resolution strategies, including alternative dispute resolution, divorce mediation, and collaborative divorce, are explored. In later chapters, we address negotiating life-changing decisions with older parents, including when to take the car keys away, moving in with an adult child, and transitioning to an assisted or senior living facility.

Each chapter looks at different situations you could encounter and uses real-life examples and case studies to illustrate how to successfully address them. Included in each chapter is how to plan, conduct, and complete a specific type of negotiation while being able to maintain or even improve the relationship between the parties. At the end of each chapter, in Lessons Learned, we summarize the key strategies, tactics, and tools you need to use to be successful.

Several negotiation-related principles and terms are repeated in a number of chapters and are used in the various negotiation examples. These include ground rules, types of power, active listening, and establishing common ground. Expanded definitions and examples of these and other terms are included in the chapters and then summarized in the glossary.

Chapters One through Three explain the principles and terms used to plan and execute a negotiation. These chapters also provide insight into how to apply these principles and best maximize their success in a negotiation. Subsequent chapters deal specifically with the various stages of parent-child and child-parent interactions. In addition, the last few chapters discuss dealing with healthcare professionals and institutions as well as business-related interactions.

When you've completed this book, we trust you will have learned that you can overcome any fear that you have regarding your ability to be successful in a negotiation, whether it is with your boss, fellow workers, friends, or especially a family member. As you experience various negotiation scenarios, you will be able to add the necessary behaviors to your toolbox. The greater variety of behaviors you acquire—the more tools you have in your toolbox—the better prepared you will be for any negotiation situation you encounter.

We hope you enjoy the journey and find at the end that you are better prepared for the challenges life holds for you.

CHAPTER ONE

Ground Rules and Ethical Behavior

Jerry has been employed at his construction firm for five years and now is one of the union shop stewards representing the finish carpenters. He has just come from a planning meeting where the executive committee has laid out its positions on each item to be bargained. This will be his first exposure to a contract negotiation with management. Jerry has heard that these negotiations can be fraught with disagreement and conflict. He has been told not to trust anything management says, and if the union doesn't get what it wants, they need to threaten to walk out and strike. Jerry questions whether this is the right approach to a difficult negotiation.

This chapter addresses many important principles, terms, and ground rules that are found in all types of negotiations and form the foundation of the planning process, which is key to any successful negotiation. Each of these principles is discussed in detail in this and in subsequent chapters, with examples of how to best apply them to a real-life situation. You will learn when and how to maximize the potential outcome for any negotiation. Your ultimate goal should be to build an ongoing collaborative relationship on a foundation of trust with the other party.

Ground Rules

There are rules that govern all negotiations, if they are going to be conducted in a fair and ethical manner, no matter what the topic is and who is involved. These "ground rules" should be clearly articulated prior to conducting any negotiation. In a family-based negotiation, each person involved knows what role each party plays. If you are the child, mom and dad have all the power, both legitimate (based on their position in the family) and informational (based on their experience and education). In many of these cases, there is no real negotiation. Until a certain age, it is understood that parents know best. As the child grows older and becomes educated and more worldly, the balance of power begins to shift. The parents are required to reduce the use of coercive types of power (threats of punishment, loud voices, and word choices) and begin to reason more with their child. Usually these so-called negotiations take place in the home, not in a neutral location.

Before beginning any negotiation, it is important to articulate the ground rules: how the participants are expected to behave in the negotiation, who speaks first, topics to be discussed, and choice of language. If you are about to play poker, you review how the game is played, including how much you can bet, the number of cards allowed per hand, and the types of poker to be played. The same approach works in a negotiation. Prior to the start of the negotiation, the parties should agree upon how the negotiation will be conducted (the ground rules) as well as other topics, which will be addressed later.

Many times in a family negotiation, the father or the mother will dominate the discussion, which then becomes one-sided. They use phrases like "you will do this" and "you will do that." As the participants become more mature and experienced, the communications are no longer unilateral and become multilateral, with all other members of the family expressing their opinions and needs. As children grow older, the word "why" finds its way into their vocabulary, and they want to express their opinion. When this happens, the parties should begin to look for common ground (areas of agreement) on which to build the negotiation. Establishing this common ground leads to the early stages of building trust and strengthens the relationship among the family members.

Morality

As children and young adults, we are taught by our parents, teachers, and religious leaders that morality is the differentiation of intentions, decisions, and actions between those that are good or right and those that are bad or wrong. Morality can be a body of standards or principles derived from a code of conduct from a particular philosophy, religion, or culture, or it can derive from a standard that a person believes should be universal. An example of ethical philosophy is the Golden Rule, "Do onto others as you would like them to do unto you." This Golden Rule should be applied to any negotiation situation, even if the other party is not behaving ethically.

Biases

Each of us needs to be aware that we tend to bring one or more "biases" into any discussion/negotiation. These are our preconceptions regarding the topic being discussed or the participants in the negotiation. There is also a tendency to believe that some people, ideas, etc., are better or worse than others. These notions usually result in treating people unfairly and can potentially damage a negotiation and, ultimately, the relationship. Whenever possible, each discussion/negotiation should be approached with an open mind and the awareness that there may be one or more biases influencing your decision-making process. When discussing/negotiating with younger children, don't generalize; treat each child as an individual with specific needs and desires.

Unethical Behaviors

A question regularly posed to us is: What motivates people to be unethical? There are a number of reasons, including the desires to:

- Compete with an opponent.
- Restore some standard of justice based on a previous interaction.

- Gain power over an opponent/partner.
- Make an easy profit.

When discussing ethics, we focus on five specific unethical behaviors that parties may engage in during the negotiation. They are *bluffing, misrepresentation, falsification, selective disclosure,* and *deception:*

Bluffing is manifested through false threats and/or a misrepresentation of the facts and the negotiation's potential outcomes. In poker, bluffing is an expected behavior and is enhanced by large initial bets and raises. In a family negotiation, however, bluffing can be demonstrated by statements such as "I won't do that again." In a business situation, a threat could be a bluff. An example could be: "If you don't treat me with more respect, I will quit." If an employee does threaten to quit, respond in a positive manner and open a discussion regarding their request for respect. Caution: To make your threat real, be sure you are ready to carry out the threat before you voice it. Following through with the "grounding" or "time out" for your child demonstrates that you are not bluffing.

Misrepresentation is a common form of unethical behavior in which the individual distorts a fact or situation. An example would be the phrase, "It was not all my fault, John also did it."

Falsification is demonstrated when parties use false information to defend their actions. They may even introduce erroneous or altered information into the conversation to defend their unethical or illegal actions. An example would be using incomplete or altered statistics that support their position.

Selective disclosure takes place when the individual does not truly communicate their wishes, desires, or position. In some instances, they will play one person against another, for example, "Mommy said it was all right."

But then you find that Mommy's approval of the child's actions was based on incomplete information. An example would be, "Can Johnny and I go for a bike ride in the neighborhood?" In reality, they rode to a destination outside their neighborhood, one that was not approved. If you desire to extinguish this behavior, remind the child that if this behavior happens again, there will be specific punishments, such as the loss of bike privileges.

Deception occurs when an individual constructs a collection of true and false arguments that would lead the other party to a wrong conclusion. An example would be, "I was there, but I was not the one who took the last piece of cake."

These five types of behavior need to be addressed and extinguished immediately when they occur. If they are ignored and/or reinforced by success, they will become part of an individual's negotiation toolbox. Only through an open and honest discussion of the problem will effective resolutions be reached. As a negotiator, your reputation precedes you; if you are viewed as unethical, that perception is difficult to change.

The goals of a family-based negotiation should include the achievement of specific objectives for both the parents and their children, such as additional income in the form of allowance, extended curfews, the use of the family car, and chores around the home. As in many business or personal negotiations, the goal is also to build communication and enhance the relationship between the parties.

Dispute versus Conflict
To better understand the circumstances under which a negotiation takes place, we need to be able to discern the difference between a "dispute" and a "conflict." Disputes involve specific issues, complaints, and frustrations

between the parties. A dispute becomes a conflict when it transitions to being personal, and when anger and blame are involved. Negotiations can take place under both circumstances, but disputes are easier to resolve than conflicts. Young children have a dispute when they both want to use the same toy or watch different programs on television. Usually the parents act as mediators and resolve the dispute by arranging a compromise between the children. When partners argue over a vacation destination or a major purchase, they have a dispute. Again, these disputes are usually resolved through compromise.

It is not unusual for the average person to confuse a dispute and a conflict. Resolving a conflict will take more time because it is more complex and involves stronger, more deep-seated emotions, such as revenge or retaliation. An example of this type of situation is when the car dealer informs you, the purchaser, that you are getting the best price possible on a car purchase, and later you find out there were "rebates" that were not offered. As a result, you may retaliate by "bad mouthing" the dealer on social media.

Many times minor childhood conflicts never get resolved—they fester and result in siblings who don't talk to each other as adults. The earlier the intervention is applied to a dispute, the less chance it will develop into a conflict and the easier it will be to negotiate a resolution. This is an important fact to be taken into consideration when planning any negotiation.

When the family owns and is involved in the running of a business entity, the types and intensity of the negotiations become susceptible to emotions influenced by previous interactions and life experiences. We have dealt with family business conflicts that were based in long-standing sibling rivalries. It is difficult for members in a family business to put these old conflicts behind when dealing with each other.

Hot Buttons

It is not unusual when a party in a negotiation elects to push your "hot buttons." These words, actions, and phrases are designed to get you off track and break your concentration or focus. Their strategy is to escalate the conflict, making it harder to achieve a resolution. We all have one or more hot buttons that trigger a response. They can be a word like "untrustworthy," which is Cary's personal hot button. The word "liar" is another common hot button. A gesture, such as pointing or shaking your finger, can be seen as an insult, resulting in an escalation in emotion. During a conflict or dispute, each of us has been known to retaliate by pushing someone else's buttons during a heated discussion or negotiation.

According to the Center for Conflict Dynamics at Eckerd College, hot buttons are those irritations and annoyances that can provoke you into conflict. These are the situations or characteristics in others that aggravate and frustrate you, perhaps to the point where, despite knowing better, you instigate a conflict. Interactions with button-pushers can leave you feeling demoralized, unmotivated, powerless, anxious, frightened, and angry (possibly enough to resort to sabotage or other destructive acts).

Responding to your hot buttons in the workplace can lead you to be less productive, efficient, organized, and creative. They can also negatively affect your life outside of work, as well as your physical and emotional well-being.

On her CoachDQ website, certified professional coach Dawn Quesnel states, "The first step toward resolving hot button issues is to understand how others impact you. . . . Unless someone is acting in an immoral manner, is violating the law, or is unethical, you need to look inward to determine what role you are playing when the conflict arises."

Strategies for defusing a conflict include:

- Take a deep breath and ask yourself why this person or situation causes you to be uncomfortable.
- Advise the other party that their behavior will not be rewarded or influence the outcome of the negotiation.
- Be aware of your own hot buttons and then turn them off. As a result, the other party may become be frustrated and change their approach.
- Refocus the discussion/negotiation back to the agreed-upon agenda items.
- Defuse the tension by taking a break.

If none of the above strategies work, reschedule the discussion/negotiation. There is no reason to continue in such a tense atmosphere, as nothing productive will be accomplished. In a business negotiation, if the behavior continues, you may wish to request that another individual represent their company. This may involve having your superior contact the other company and request the change in representation. Don't retaliate by pushing their hot buttons, which would only escalate the level of conflict and be destructive to the relationship.

Building Trust

Trust is the basis of any relationship, and a major component of it. In a negotiation scenario, trusting that your negotiating counterpart (partner) will execute what they commit to in a negotiation is critical to its success. In a negotiation, the parties work to build trust, the foundation for any long-term relationship. Building trust takes time and is based on the reputation and experience of prior dealings between these negotiators. In order to build this trust, both parties need to clearly communicate, collaborate, and compromise to accomplish the agreed-upon goals. In some instances contracts are used to facilitate trust, with consequences for non-performance.

Once trust is lost, the relationship is put at risk and the negotiation will ultimately fail. As stated earlier, sometimes a relationship can be repaired by just changing the players. In a family relationship, you don't have that option; you cannot change the members of your family. Rebuilding trust will take time and require a change in approach and attitude.

SMART Goals

The goals identified in a negotiation should be **SMART**: **S**pecific, **M**easurable, **A**ttainable, **R**ealistic, and **T**imely. SMART goals as they relate to a child's academic achievement are something all parents should be concerned with during their child's journey from kindergarten through high school. These types of goals should be tailored to the child's ability to comprehend, learn, and process information.

For example, a SMART goal specific for a middle school child could be to complete their homework assignments each night by 9:00 p.m. This goal would need to be based on the amount of homework usually assigned and the ability of the child to organize and complete the work in the allotted time. Depending on the type of homework assigned, the time frame and the level of parent involvement would vary. As parents review these SMART goals with their child during the school year, they need to be open to the possibility that assistance may be required that they cannot provide. Parents may then consider whether outside assistance will help the child accomplish the goals that were agreed to at the beginning. This assistance can take the form of tutoring from another student or a professional tutor, additional time after school with a teacher, or support made available through another institution, including an online one.

Flexibility is important in any negotiation, because the components considered in the decision process can vary each time you meet with your child. Rigidity is your enemy in these situations, because homework assignments vary in their complexity as the school year progresses and as the grade levels change. You will need to revisit your agreed-upon goals each term and at each grade level for them to remain relevant and actionable.

Agenda

If possible, especially in a business setting, an agenda should be published prior to the negotiation/discussion with sufficient time for the parties to properly respond and formulate their negotiation strategies.

Sophisticated negotiators will try to control the agenda and will disclose or withhold strategic information to best suit their own ends. In collaborative negotiations, share more; in competitive negotiations, share less.

In Chapter Two, "Planning and Executing Your Negotiation," we demonstrate how to assemble your information and develop a negotiating plan. Preparation is the key to a successful execution. The more time you spend planning, the less time you will spend negotiating and executing the agreement. In each preparation session, you should be assembling information that will support your position and the achievement of your goals. You need to consider your goals, their goals, and the type of power you will elect to use to convince the other party that your position and solutions are valid. You should also identify possible concessions that you would be willing to make in order to achieve your identified goals. Negotiation is a process of give and take. In Chapter Two, we discuss these terms and strategies in depth.

Generational Issues in a Family Business

In Chapter Eleven, "Negotiating in a Business Setting," we delve into the types of negotiations that are involved in a family business. The goal of these negotiations is to maintain harmony within the family and the generations while running a successful business. This is a lofty goal, considering the 50 percent failure rate of family businesses from one generation to another. The history of many family-owned businesses is fraught with tension and anger among the siblings, which produces a toxic work environment and endangers the success of the enterprise.

Opening Statement

We have been asked many times who should go first in a negotiation. The answer is, "It depends." If you have sufficient information, then you may elect to go first. A question to be pondered is: "Do I gain a strategic advantage by going first?" In some business situations, Cary has seen a coin flip used to determine who speaks first. In other cases, like a family meeting, the individual who initiated the meeting should probably speak first.

One of our favorite strategies is to let the other person initiate the negotiation process. Usually in their opening comments, the other party will reveal their desired outcomes for the negotiation and other pertinent information. This strategy permits you to restructure your opening statement and to respond to their desired outcomes with counter proposals. It will also demonstrate that you "heard" them, respect them, and are using "active listening" techniques. These listening techniques are explained in detail in subsequent chapters.

You now have entered the world of negotiation. Your journey continues with the next chapter, in which we discuss how to plan and execute a successful negotiation. You will discover that you cannot use a "cookie cutter" approach to a negotiation and that you will need to understand the interests, goals, and emotions of the other party in order to satisfy your own interests. Everyone has a different view of what is an acceptable outcome. Only through research, communication, and listening carefully to the other party will you reach a "win-win" outcome. The following chapter deals with the planning process and discusses how to gain an "EDGE" over the other party when planning for and executing your next negotiation.

Lessons Learned

- Ground rules regarding expected behavior should be articulated prior to the start of any negotiation. The participants must be aware of which behaviors will be accepted and which ones will be not tolerated.

- No one should dominate the negotiation. All individuals should have equal opportunities to state their case clearly and respond to the other party's offers and requests set forth in the opening statement.

- Be aware of unethical behaviors, such as bluffing, misrepresentation, falsification, selective disclosure, and deception. When these behaviors are demonstrated in a negotiation, don't ignore them. You need to call the other party on these types of behaviors in order to extinguish them. These behaviors are adopted to gain power over the other party.

- Understand the difference between a dispute and a conflict. Disputes can usually be resolved quickly, while a conflict, which is usually more emotionally based, requires more research, energy, and time.

- Don't let people break your concentration or derail the negotiation through the use of "hot buttons." Be prepared for that tactic and don't react. Identify your hot buttons and cognitively turn them off. Pushing a hot button is a "power play" designed to get you off task. Stay focused on the task at hand; this will signal the other party that their disruptive tactics are not working.

- Trust is a major component of any negotiation and is built over time. Trust is earned by the successful completion of the negotiated agreement. Trust is lost when the parties to a negotiation do not perform as agreed upon in the negotiation. Once lost, trust is difficult to rebuild and will take time.

- Always try to include **SMART** (**S**pecific, **M**easurable, **A**ttainable, **R**ealistic, and **T**imely) goals in your negotiation planning. By including these types of goals, you will be able to accurately assess whether your goals are accomplished within a reasonable time frame.

- If possible, an agenda should be published prior to the negotiation/ discussion with sufficient time so the parties can properly respond and formulate their negotiation strategies.

CHAPTER TWO

Planning and Executing Your Negotiation

After their initial bargaining session with management, Jerry, the newest member of the bargaining committee, realizes that his union did not develop any alternatives to their original contract proposals. As a result, when management countered with its proposal, the union was not prepared to accept it or offer an alternative. The union's proposals were based on information provided to them by the international union office in New York. This information did not reflect the prevailing wages and benefits in their local's district. They could not properly support their proposals with the information the union office in New York had provided. The result was an impasse.

Poor planning leads to poor results. Proper planning is the key to a successful negotiation, no matter what topic is being discussed. Negotiators who are successful constantly work at improving their preparation, organization, communication, and execution skills. They also know that it is unusual to attain all your goals in a negotiation, and they should be prepared to deal and compromise in order to maximize the results. We find the "80/20 rule" valuable: if you spend 80 percent of your time planning, you will spend 20 percent on execution and obtain a better outcome. This chapter provides you with planning, communication, and other skills as well as an understanding of how each gender typically approaches a negotiation. In addition, we look at how culture impacts a negotiation.

First, let's look at an approach to planning that would give you an EDGE in your next negotiation.

Gaining an EDGE

Using the acronym "EDGE," which was developed by Cary in 2008, can improve your negotiating outcomes no matter what the situation or topic. Each letter of **EDGE** can contribute to a successful negotiation outcome:

Educate yourself about the opposition and their interests.

- Research the individual or individuals with whom you will be negotiating. Use Google, Ask, Dogpile, Bing, or other search engines to get the latest information on the individuals and their activities. If you are negotiating with a caterer regarding a wedding, for example, find out what other caterers charge or ask friends about the caterers they have used for special events.

- Review the history of the relationship. What was the content of the last contact? Have you negotiated with this individual before? What was the result of the last negotiation? In the case of your child, have you had this conversation before? Is there a precedent? You need to review what transpired, and the content and results of the previous negotiation. Based on those results, you have a starting point for the next phase of negotiation and the ability to maintain a consistent message.

- These questions address the state of the relationship: Were there any problems with implementation? Have any bridges been burned and can they be rebuilt? Is the relationship fractured and in need of repair? Is it dormant and needs to be reactivated, or is it ongoing? The state of the relationship will determine your initial strategies.

- Assemble a two-column list on a single piece of paper with your interests and those of your negotiating counterpart side by side. After assembling this list, begin to prioritize your interests. This is an important exercise that will come in handy during the negotiation.

- Once this list is prioritized, look for parallel interests (the common ground) and use them as the "jumping off" point for the negotiation.

You should also identify potential areas of disagreement. You will need to develop strategies to turn negatives into positives. For example, when negotiating a wedding contract, the caterer may require a large deposit, and you feel that the amount is too high. You may offer the alternative of paying a smaller deposit in advance and an equal amount just prior to the wedding to slow the pace of your out-of-pocket expenses.

• Identify which interests you would surrender in order to achieve agreement on the balance of your interests. You can achieve this by ranking your interests from most important to least important. Those at the bottom can be offered as concessions and should always be linked to a concession the other party may offer. For example, "I will do this if you will do that." Linking is an integral part of any negotiation. Always be aware of situations where linking is possible. Once the opportunity for linking is missed, it is difficult to relink concessions later in a negotiation.

Develop a BATNA, ZOPA, and WATNA.

• Your **BATNA** is your **B**est **A**lternative **T**o a **N**egotiated **A**greement. These are the other possible agreements that are available to you. You need to have at least one **BATNA** prior to starting any negotiation. An example: negotiating an eleven o'clock curfew with your teenager, knowing that you will accept a midnight curfew.

• The **ZOPA** is the **Z**one **O**f **P**otential **A**greement. The ZOPA is divided into three sections: aspire to, content with, and live with. You want a deal that falls within the middle, or the "content with," section of your ZOPA. Eighty percent of all negotiations are settled in this section of the ZOPA. In a negotiation that has multiple goals, you may achieve "aspire to" for one or more goals, "content with" for a majority, and even "live with" for some goals. This is the essence of a "win-win" negotiation scenario.

• It is important that you know your **WATNA**, your **W**orst **A**lternative **T**o a **N**egotiated **A**greement. This prevents you from agreeing to a deal that is not acceptable, one that you must "live with." This is the wrong end of your ZOPA. An example of a WATNA is accepting an open-ended curfew or allowing your elderly parent to drive even if he drives in an unsafe manner. You also need to consider the consequences of not reaching an agreement. More than one professional negotiator has commented, "No agreement is better than a bad agreement." Sometimes you just need to walk away.

Gather the necessary data to support your interests in the negotiation.

- All the pertinent information and statistics that will support your view of the situation and diffuse potential objections should be gathered. Make sure your data are current and pertinent. For example, if you are preparing to buy a car, gather information on the prices and the equipment you desire. Find out about any dealer rebates, if possible. Visiting more than one dealership will give you an opportunity to negotiate the best deal and develop a BATNA.

  In many cases, the data you need is found in business, family, medical, or public records. Profit-and-loss statements, wills, financial records, medical history, and other web-based information can form the basis of your negotiation.

- Whenever possible, you should consult with experts. This is particularly critical when dealing with older adults, where you may elect to speak with their physician or therapist to gather the necessary health-related information. The same strategy holds true for adolescent children. Getting insights from a family or adolescent therapist could be of great benefit, providing insights into teen behavior and aiding in formulating your strategies.

Execute your plan and then evaluate your performance.

- Plan your negotiation while developing an agenda that details who will be responsible for presenting each side's interests. Practice time management by assigning time frames to each person's presentation.

- Publish the agenda in advance of the meeting and ask for comments. By publishing the agenda, you publicly commit each participant to being prepared for the meeting. By asking for feedback, you can adjust the agenda to meet the needs of both parties. This is your first step toward a collaborative agreement.

- Have an opening statement prepared that articulates your interests and also demonstrates an understanding of their interests and the content of the negotiation. Don't be afraid to revise your opening statement and your strategy based upon the other side's opening statement. This will demonstrate that you are "actively listening."

- Prioritize your interests. People "expect concessions," so have them identified and be ready to offer them in order to achieve your major negotiating goals. You should expect reciprocal concessions in the form of counter proposals, but don't bid against yourself and give away value. Compromising sets a tone of cooperation and helps build relationships.

- Link any concession that you offer to an interest that you need satisfied. All negotiations involve give and take. There is nothing wrong in requesting that the other side meet you halfway when you are offering a concession. You have the option of accepting or rejecting it.

- Review your two-column list and see if your interests have been satisfied. If there are unsatisfied interests, you should put them on the table and discuss them, or agree to discuss them at a future time. Try not to leave any "value" on the table. Be sure you have discussed all items on your list before you conclude the negotiation.

- Summarize the results of the negotiation in writing and ask the other party if there are any additions or corrections that need to be made.

- Address any open issues and ask for feedback from the other party on how to resolve them before finalizing the agreement. Understand that once the agreement is consummated, it will be more difficult to resolve any open issues.

- If any open issue that is important to the other side has been omitted, you may elect to reopen the negotiation and let them "save face" with their superiors. This will provide you with an "IOU" for a future negotiation. The same strategy applies to personal or family negotiation scenarios.

By using the **EDGE** model, you can approach your next negotiation with a renewed level of confidence, a higher level of preparation, and knowledge of the issues and strategies that will permit you to reach your personal negotiating goals.

Using Power

Power is a major component in any negotiation. In many negotiations, the person who has the greatest power prevails.

Let's review each type of power and how it can impact a negotiation.

- *Associative power* is derived from whom you know or are associated with, both inside and outside of an organization. An example is when a father and son in a family business form an alliance to fight off an initiative from another family member in the business. The father and son would gain additional associative power over the other family member by aligning themselves with a major stockholder in the company.

- *Coercive power* is derived from using negative behaviors such as threats and bullying, or from a person's position in a family, organization, or business. Anyone can choose to use coercive power, but doing so is destructive to long-term relationships.

- *Economic power* is having the ability to influence a decision by threatening to withhold funds or labor. A partner who has a majority share of stock in a business would be afforded this type of power.

- *Expert power* is a form of information power and brings a high level of stature to the person perceived as an expert. Examples of experts include psychologists, physicians, lawyers, and scientists.

- *Information power* is accorded to individuals who have the ability to accumulate large amounts of data on a specific topic. In a family-owned business, a portion of this information may relate to the history of the organization, how decisions are made, and who makes them.

- *Legitimate power* is based on an individual's position in an organization. Individuals who hold "C"-level positions (CEO, CFO, CIO, and COO) in a business have legitimate power simply by nature of their titles. In a family setting, birth order is another source of legitimate power.

Now let's address a skill set that separates good negotiators from great ones. The skill is the art of active listening.

Active Listening

To actively listen, you need to overcome some barriers. It is not uncommon when negotiating with someone to be thinking on two planes. The brain has the ability to process multiple thoughts simultaneously. In order to focus on what someone is saying, you must temporarily suspend all unrelated thoughts. By doing this, you are learning to manage what goes on in your mind.

Let your negotiating counterpart know you are listening by responding with verbal and nonverbal cues, including facial expressions and short phrases such as, "I hear your concerns." Another strategy is to provide verbal feedback in the form of brief statements that focus on the key words and issues. You may choose to paraphrase what others are saying to ensure that you understanding them correctly. They should respond with clarifying statements if your paraphrasing is not accurate.

For example, your college professor requests that you lead the next day's class discussion on the underlying causes of the Second World War in Europe. You paraphrase your response as follows: "You want me to lead the class in discussing the economic, political, and social changes that formed the basis of the unrest that led to the start of the Second World War in Europe." In this manner, you have actively focused the discussion and clarified what you will be speaking about. This action will reduce any possible misunderstanding when your teacher agrees with your response.

You can support or challenge what your negotiating partner is saying by adding your thoughts to their insights. If you are not totally clear on what they are communicating, encourage further explanation in a respectful manner.

By listening actively, you ensure that what is communicated is clear to both parties, which reduces the potential for misunderstandings. The ten steps outlined in this next section will further sharpen your listening skills:

Ten Steps to Better Communication Skills

"What we've got here is failure to communicate" is one of the most famous movie lines from *Cool Hand Luke,* starring Paul Newman and Strother Martin. It is representative of many daily conversations between individuals. One person believes her message is clear in its content, but the other person's understanding in no way reflects the intended message.

Let's look at ten steps that will help focus your communication so that the potential for misunderstanding is significantly reduced. These steps were originally identified in the article "Ten Commandments of Good Communication" by the American Management Association in 1961.

1. Clarify your ideas before communicating.

    Many communications/negotiations fail due to inadequate planning and because we don't fully consider the goals and attitudes of those who are involved in the process. In many situations, we also fail to consider those who will be affected by what we are saying.

Example:

> Former Wisconsin Governor Tommy Thompson once made a comment at a fundraiser about a group of ethnic businessmen that he thought was funny. Many of that same ethnic group in the audience found his comments offensive. He ended up apologizing for his comments. He should have considered the impact on others of using stereotypic statements.

Tools to use:

- Draft an outline of the communication in advance and review it with your peers. Be ready to make changes that will sharpen the message.

- Confine the communication to one or two relevant goals in order to bring better focus to your efforts.

- Consider whether others will be affected by this communication and consider the impact of your words on them.

2.   Examine the true purpose of each communication.

Identify your most important goal for each communication. It will require you to adapt your language, tone, and approach to serve that specific goal. Remember, the sharper the focus of your message, the greater its chance of success.

Example:

A communication that begins with an aggressive tone and with language that is viewed as abusive will not be openly received. The audience will be immediately turned off by the tone and choice of words. They will not hear the rest of the intended message. This negative response can be avoided by opening with a positive comment. Now the audience will cue in to the balance of the message. This negotiation technique of beginning a communication with a positive tone is called "anchoring."

Tools to use:

• Determine what changes you desire behaviorally from your target audience and focus your communication on those behaviors.

• Beware of your tone; be assertive, not aggressive or arrogant.

• Choose your language carefully; your words can betray your intent.

3.   Consider the total physical and human setting whenever you communicate.

The meaning and intent of a communication is conveyed by more than words. We must take into consideration the "physical setting," the "social climate," and "custom and past practice" among the participants. The communication must be appropriate to its environment.

Example:

As the presidential candidates move from state to state, they change their language, their approach, and even their clothing to adapt to the environment in which they are speaking. In Iowa, the candidates focus on the issues that impact the farmers, such as ethanol and farm subsidies, and they may wear jeans and a denim work shirt. As they move into the larger industrial states, the focus switches to protecting jobs, the minimum wage, and healthcare issues; there they wear a suit and tie.

Tools to use:

- Where you hold your meeting or deliver your message can determine how it is interpreted by the other party. For example, a parent-child negotiation may be quite different if held in the child's bedroom rather than the living or dining room, where the child would feel the conversation was more formal and the topic more serious. Similarly, holding a meeting in your office (the power of the office) sends a different signal than holding it in a neutral location.

- Who attends the meeting also sends a message to the receiver. Be careful whom you invite to the meeting.

4. Consult with others when appropriate in planning communications.
    Consulting with others prior to starting a negotiation often helps to lend additional insight and objectivity to your message. In addition, the individuals who assisted in the planning process will be more apt to provide their active support when the message is delivered.

Example:

When a firm announces a new strategic alliance or acquisition, it should be presented in such a way that it appears that both firms had equal input into the agreement and the announcement.

When parents announce to their family that they are moving to a new home or having a new baby, they should deliver the message jointly.

Tools to use:

- Go over the exhibits and handouts that you plan to use in your negotiation with your colleagues to see how they interpret the materials.

- Adjust your materials and communication strategy based on their feedback.

- Where possible, incorporate their words into your presentation to demonstrate respect for their input.

5. It is important to be aware of the overtones as well as the basic content of your message.

   The subtleties of a communication often impact/affect a listener's reaction to a message even more than its basic content. Many times the choice of language determines, in large part, the reactions of your audience. Because of the diversity of today's workforce, this step should be given careful consideration.

   Example:

   > If you have a bilingual workforce, make announcements not only in English but also in the workers' native language. When addressing non-English-speaking audiences, be sure that an interpreter is consulted so that the translation into the other language is accurate. Often phrases from one language do not translate accurately into other languages. This pertains particularly to cross-cultural negotiations, where an interpreter is needed to accurately translate complicated communications.

   Tools to use:

   - Know your audience; use the correct vocabulary level when speaking with them. Don't speak over their heads or insult their level of intelligence; stay away from "corporate speak," jargon, and word choices that might imply that you are "talking down" to them.

   - Avoid generalities, words, or phrases that could be misinterpreted, especially when dealing with individuals from other cultures.

   - Prior to making your presentation, gain insights by speaking with someone from that culture or ethnic group. Attempt to eliminate words or phrases that might lead to a misunderstanding.

6. Take the opportunity to convey something of help or value to the receiver.

   When composing your communication, it is critical to consider the other person's needs and interests. It is to your advantage to look at things from their point of view—"walk in their shoes," as they say. It is import-ant to convey something of immediate benefit or long-range value in your initial communication. You don't want them to walk away thinking, "I wonder what he is really up to?"

Example:

> Prior to interviewing for a new position, be sure to do your research as to the firm's various markets, their products, and their competition. This will permit you to start the interview in a positive manner by demonstrating that you have knowledge of the firm, its products, its history, its challenges, and how your skills can assist them with the achievement of their goals. An example of a positive anchor would be: "In reviewing the history of your company, I was struck by the fact that you are a leader in this segment of the industry."

Tools to use:

- You may elect to use the "anchoring technique," discussed earlier, where you begin your conversation with a positive thought so that the audience will be drawn to your message.

- Know that when you use a positive anchor in the beginning of your statement, it softens the impact of anything negative that may follow.

- Address the other party's concerns as well as your own; this will reduce resistance to your message.

7. Follow up on your communication.

A very important step is following up on how your message was per-ceived. Ask the other party if there is any additional information they may need in order to make a decision. Probing may expose areas of mis-understanding or gaps in the communication and permit you to clarify and share additional information.

Example:

> When conducting a performance appraisal with an employee who is having challenges, you need to schedule

a thirty-day follow-up meeting after the initial performance appraisal. This will permit you to see if the requested changes in behavior are taking place and if any clarification is required. Employ active listening techniques and open-ended questions to challenge the employee to fully respond during the initial and follow-up conferences.

Tools to use:

- Pose "open-ended" questions, ones that require detailed responses and that encourage the receiver to express their reaction with a more than a simple "yes" or "no." Open-ended questions collect information and usually include words such as *who, what, when, how,* or *why.*

- Ask others to demonstrate that they understand the communication by re-phrasing in their own words what you said (an active listening technique).

- In order to receive feedback, follow-up with one or more contacts with that individual. Also review their subsequent performance on agreed-upon objectives.

8. Communicate for tomorrow as well as today.

It is important to plan your communication with the future in mind. You need to be consistent with your long-range interests and goals. The person you are communicating with should have an idea of what to expect from you. There is a good chance you will be communicating and negotiating with the same individual in the future.

Example:

> As an employer, you don't want to make a presentation to your employees promising actions that you have failed to complete in the past. Be sure to address any unmet promises prior to committing to any future actions. The famous "read my lips" speech President George H. W. Bush made regarding the raising of taxes became an embarrassment when he needed to raise taxes at a future date. Since he previously committed to not raise taxes, he lost his credibility with the American voters and his bid for reelection to Bill Clinton.

Tools to use:

- Review previous communications/negotiations to ensure that you are consistent with past practices.

- Where necessary, speak with previous negotiators to gain insights into the behavior of the other party.

- Neutralize any past commitments not executed by previous negotiators by acknowledging them and committing to prevent any reoccurrence.

- Explain what actions have been taken to correct those situations so they will no longer be of concern to the other party.

9. Your actions need to support your communications.

   Employees will closely watch your actions to see if they contradict your words. You need to be consistent in both your words and your actions.

Example:

> Explaining to your employees that expenses need to be cut and that salary increases will be at the minimum because of low profits and then giving bonuses to management is a poor practice. This happened when Northwest Airlines asked their pilots and flight attendants to provide givebacks but then issued bonuses to their executives. As a result, the level of trust between the parties was seriously damaged.

Tools to use:

- Don't fall into the trap of "Don't do what I do, do what I say."

- Be sure the actions of your management team do not contradict your statements.

10. Seek not only to be understood but also to understand. Be a good listener.

    One of the most important, most difficult, and most neglected skills in communication is listening.

Example:

> When making a presentation, encourage your audience
> to ask questions after the presentation is completed. The
> questions that are asked will demonstrate the audience's
> level of understanding. You may need to clarify one or
> more of your points as a result of the questions posed. This
> constructive feedback will permit you to adjust future
> presentations and increase their effectiveness.

Tools to use:

- Use "active listening" techniques to measure the level of understanding
  within the audience. This also provides you the opportunity to clarify
  your message.

- Cary's mother always stated, "You have two ears and one mouth. Use
  them in proportion."

If you follow these ten steps, you will find that the chances of failing
to communicate will diminish greatly, and you will be more effective in
achieving your goals.

Lessons Learned

- Find common ground as quickly as possible by exchanging a list of needs and desired outcomes prior to the negotiation. Once common ground is identified, use it as your "jumping off" point.

- Compose your opening statement in a manner that acknowledges the other side's interests while stressing your own. Prepare an agenda that incorporates the interests of both parties.

- You will increase your chances for success by using the **EDGE** (**E**ducate, **D**evelop, **G**ather, **E**xecute) approach to planning your next negotiation. Make sure that you identify your **BATNA** (**B**est **A**lternative **T**o a **N**egotiated **A**greement), **ZOPA** (**Z**one **O**f **P**otential **A**greement), and **WATNA** (**W**orst **A**lternative **T**o a **N**egotiated **A**greement) prior to entering into the negotiation.

- Consider using "power" in your negotiation to leverage the perception of the situation and the possible solutions suggested.

- Actively listening to your negotiating partner will increase your potential for success. When you have an accurate picture of what the other person is trying to accomplish, you can better organize and strategize. Active listening acknowledges the other side's message and gives it validity.

- Be sure to use "open-ended" questions when seeking information or clarification of issues. Closed-ended questions receive a "yes" or "no" answer, while "open-ended" questions collect information and usually include words such as, *who, what, when, how,* or *why.*

- Remember that you are not only negotiating, but you are also building trust and a relationship with the other party. Your behavior in this negotiation will impact future negotiations and your reputation.

- In a business-related negotiation, if the other party makes a mistake, don't take advantage; let the other party "save face" and correct the mistake. Remember, you are not only negotiating for today but for tomorrow. Saving face also creates an "IOU" for future negotiations.

Chapter Three

Understanding Gender and Cultural Differences

In the 1980s, a successful American oil company won a contract to build a refinery in a Middle Eastern country. It brought in experienced construction crews from Europe and other Western countries. After the refinery was completed and ready to begin production, trailers were set up to interview prospective employees. After two weeks, the company was frustrated because they could not find a single person interested in working at the refinery. A local businessman came forward and informed them that unless the local tribal leader gave his approval to their project, no member of the tribe would apply for a job. The refinery managers requested a meeting with the local tribal leader and negotiated a tribute. They returned to their offices the next day and found a long line of men waiting to apply for work.

B efore you enter into a negotiation in a foreign country, you must consider the culture as you develop your plan. In this chapter, we discuss how to prepare for the differences in the approach to a negotiation based on gender and culture. The mantra here is "no two people negotiate or communicate in the same manner." Together we can explore those differences and learn how to obtain better outcomes. Understand, however, that gender and culture are not reliable predictors of negotiation performance across all situations.

Gender Differences

Researchers have found that men and women approach a negotiation differently. We all are aware that people are different, but there are similar characteristics found in each gender's approach to a negotiation. Cary and other academics, including Dr. Yasmin Davidds of UCLA, have conducted interviews, administered questionnaires, and reviewed secondary research as they endeavored to understand and isolate the differences in the approach and execution of a negotiation by men and women.

Before you begin planning and conducting a negotiation, you need to understand who you are dealing with and their tendencies. To be successful in a negotiation, gender-specific differences need to be explored and understood to prevent surprises in your efforts to reach an agreement.

According to the research by Dina W. Pradel, Hannah Riley Bowles, and Kathleen L. McGinn, reported in an article in the February 2006 Harvard Business School newsletter *Working Knowledge* titled "When Gender Changes the Negotiation," gender is not a reliable predictor of negotiation performance. Neither women nor men perform better or worse across all negotiations. However, certain situations can set the stage for differences in outcomes negotiated by men and by women, particularly when:

1. The opportunities and limits of the negotiation are unclear.
2. Something is happening in the environment that is interpreted as needing a response (situational cue).
3. Situational cues signal that the person needs to respond in particular ways.

During a negotiation, there are marked differences in how women and men communicate. Historically, women have been portrayed as the weaker sex in movies and in literature. If a man takes only that interpretation of a woman's behavior into a negotiation, he will be surprised and find himself at quite a disadvantage. It is dangerous to generalize behavior. Just like men, not all women behave the same way in a negotiation. When evaluating a potential negotiating counterpart, experience, education, and personality are all important variables that need to be considered in addition to gender.

Women in a Negotiation

- On average, women are not as distributive (concerned with winning) as males but are more collaborative (concerned with building the relationship) in their approach to a negotiation.
- According to Yasmin Davidds, PsyD, in her 2015 book *On Your Own Terms: A Woman's Guide to Taking Charge of Any Negotiation,* women want to know whether they can trust their negotiating partner.
- Women are more apt to accommodate the other party in a negotiation. As stated by Davidds, "Women want everyone to get along."
- When the negotiation gets heated, women are more likely to withdraw than offer a compromise.

Comments submitted by women in pre-seminar and graduate classes conducted by Cary between 1989 and 2014 support this propensity to withdraw:

- "If I am not comfortable with the person(s) on the other side of the negotiation, I will resort to a 'yes man' mode and be a bit of a pushover."
- "I give in far too easily because I do not like causing conflict."
- "I am perceived as a pushover, I think, because I don't like for conflict to be an ongoing thing."
- "I don't handle conflict well. I usually need to step away from a situation that is getting close to conflict."
- "I normally walk away from the situation in order to let both parties have time to think about the situation."

In her article "Negotiating through the Glass Ceiling," which appeared in the June 2008 newsletter *EurekAlert,* Dr. Yael Itzhaki, of Tel Aviv University, stated that she found that women may be more skilled at business negotiations than their masculine counterparts. Dr. Itzhaki carried out simulations of business negotiations among 554 Israeli and American management students at Ohio State University, in New York City, and in Israel. Dr. Itzhaki found that "women are more generous negotiators, better co-operators, and are motivated to create win-win situations." The results reported in her PhD thesis indicated that in certain groupings, women offered better terms than men to reach an agreement and women were good at facilitating interaction between the parties.

Dr. Itzhaki said women have unique skills to offer:

- They're great listeners, they care about the concerns of the other side, and they're generally more interested in finding a win-win situation to the benefit of both parties.

- Female negotiators score lower on the defeat (win-lose) scale than male negotiators, which was confirmed by Cary's research.

- Women are more concerned with substance and creating an agreement in which both parties experience a positive outcome and a relationship is maintained.

Susan Pravda, a managing partner of the Boston law office of Foley & Lardner, referenced a 1995 book by Connie Glaser and Barbara Steinberg Smalley in an article she published on the firm's website. The book was titled *Swim With the Dolphins: How Women Can Succeed in Corporate America on Their Own Terms.* In the article, Pravda strongly asserted that women have an edge over men at the negotiating table. "We can be more accessible as people, instantly. We usually have a greater ability to befriend the other side and, quite frankly, I think most people enjoy the difference. They get a kick out of the fact that it's not business-as-usual."

Ms. Pravda shared that her advantage is that, "like most women, she schmoozes pretty well." So it's easier for her to break the ice and build a better rapport with people. Also, she has found that a lot of men actually find it easier to talk to women.

Ms. Pravda thinks that she brings three major strengths to the negotiating table:

- She tends to be very creative, which is a key to solving problems that arise in a negotiation.

- She is tough, but not in a way that is characteristically considered "male toughness." She takes tough positions and tries to represent her clients to the fullest extent of her abilities.

- The final skill that she believes is critical to success, is her ability to listen. "I've learned both from personal experience and from training a lot of young associates when to stop talking and when to start listening."

As we have shared, active listening is a critical skill for successful negotiation. In our experience, we have found that women tend to be better listeners than their male counterparts. It appears that men are usually thinking of the next question and not carefully listening to the answer to their current question.

Women do a better job of advocating for others than for themselves. Women benefit when they approach negotiations in entirely different ways than do men. The differences already outlined will often give female negotiators an edge.

Men need to better understand how women prepare and execute negotiations. By doing this, men will be able to achieve better results and develop stronger relationships with their female counterparts in a business negotiation situation.

In 2000, Sandra Beckwith published an article on her website, www.sandrabeckwith.com, titled "How Can Men and Women Communicate

Better with Each Other?" In it, she suggested five tips that permit men to better communicate with women. They are:

- Understand that women communicate to establish relationships, so they might be chattier and more personal in their conversations.

- Be aware that not every question from a woman is a problem begging for a solution. Before you jump in with help, be certain she's asked for your help. Sometimes she just wants to blow off steam.

- Don't be frustrated by the fact that women use twice as many words as do men.

- Listen three times more than you would to another man.

- Get chattier, especially on the phone. You'll win her over for sure.

Now that you understand that there are distinct differences in communication patterns between men and women, you can better prepare for an upcoming negotiation or critical business conversation.

Women and Backlash

Yasmin Davidds, PsyD, in her book *On Your Own Terms: A Woman's Guide to Taking Charge of Any Negotiation*, discussed the concept of "backlash." This occurs when women behave in the same manner as men. They can be labeled unfairly, perceived as aggressive, selfish, and "bitchy" by opponents of either gender. This perception can lead to backlash, and cause women to hesitate to negotiate in an aggressive manner. Dr. Davidds indicated what issues can be included in backlash:

- Harshly evaluating a women's negotiating skills
- Less willingness to hire and work with women for a job that includes negotiation
- Viewing such a woman as a threat to traditional stereotypes

Dr. Davidds stated that when negotiating with a man, a woman needs to show him that she understands the issues and is working with him at his level. She must come across as a knowledgeable opponent. Other strategies she suggests women use are:

- Be aware of gender-related triggers, such as highly competitive behaviors by men, in single-issue negotiations. Foresee situations that may trigger gender stereotypes or role expectations and try to neutralize them.

- Do your homework. Learn as much as you can about what is possible and ask for whatever you need.

- In your opening statement, create transparency by clarifying the range of issues that are up for negotiation.

- Convey performance expectations by clearly stating your performance goals. Setting high but reasonable aspirations is good for all negotiators.

- Be mindful of the role of gender-based expectations (assumptions about how men and women should act in a negotiation).

Dr. Davidds also discussed the issue of impression management. She proposed that it is important for women to control the image that other people have of a female negotiator. This can be achieved by a woman honing the ability to control, monitor, and manage the impression she makes. Dr. Davidds recommended paying attention to these three elements:

- *Language*: The words you use can impress people or put them off. For example, use "we" and "us" instead of "I" when communicating with the other negotiator. Both "we" and "us" are equally powerful, since you are communicating that it is a joint effort to solve the problem at hand.

- *Tone*: The way you sound influences the impression you make. Use a strong yet pleasant tone when communicating with other people.

- *Framing*: How you convey your thoughts will influence how people perceive you. Consider framing the negotiation as if you were advocating on the behalf of your team and or someone else, not just yourself.

It should be noted that these three elements also work well for men.

Dr. Davidds suggested using a "sandwich technique" when framing your communication. This is similar to the "anchoring," discussed in an earlier chapter, in that you first say something nice or positive to the other person and show appreciation for their accomplishments or how they have helped or assisted you. Next, ask for what you desire and why. Lastly, complete the sandwich by explaining how the granting of your request will benefit the person and their organization.

Men in a Negotiation

Research Cary performed between 1989 and 2014 with his negotiation seminar participants and with the students in his Keller Graduate School of Management negotiating class, revealed a number of similarities and differences between the genders. Having discussed how women negotiate, it is important to discuss how men perform the same task. When preparing to negotiate with the male gender, one needs to understand how they prepare, approach, and execute a negotiation.

- Men are more "goal oriented" than women and invest a great deal of time in preparation. They tend to approach a negotiation in a "distributive" manner, concerning themselves with the distribution of results, the "who got what" from the negotiation.

- Men tend to play the zero-sum (win/lose) game. They view an accommodation as a sign of weakness and as a potential loss.

- Men are more concerned than women about the results than the relationship. They see relationships as secondary.

- Men are often considering their next move rather than listening to the other party.

- Men prefer to stick to their game plan. They adjust less nimbly to new situations than women but can adjust as long as they "win."

- Men are "tellers" not "askers."

- With regard to "risk," men are more likely to take risks than women, and aggression is the preferred mode of behavior. When negotiations heat up, men tend to dig in rather than back down.

- Men are more effective in advocating for themselves, whereas women are known to advocate better for others.

Neutralizing Gender Differences

No matter which gender is on the other side of the table, you need to be aware and consider how they will prepare, approach, and execute a negotiation. Because of experience and personality, there will be differences from person to person. You need to do your homework and talk to others about how a specific individual approaches, conducts, and behaves in a negotiation. Using the strategies laid out in this chapter will permit you to bridge and neutralize the gender gap. A key tool in your toolbox is "active listening," which we described in Chapter Two. We will further discuss how to use this communication tool in a negotiation in subsequent chapters.

Cross-cultural Negotiations

Culture is defined as a set of shared and enduring meanings, values, and behaviors. Culture can be viewed as an onion, with many layers of important beliefs and values that can have a strong influence on behavior. Culture can also be clearly ordered, which means it has a more pronounced effect on behavior because members of the organization are sure which values should prevail in cases of conflicting interests. Culture is the social adhesive that binds people together and gives them an identity as a community.

When we travel to other countries or entertain guests from other cultures, we are engaged in inter-cultural or cross-cultural negotiations. Even within the borders of the United States, we are engaged in intra-cultural negotiations. For example, people on the east coast will generally approach a negotiation differently than people in the south. These types of negotiations can be more complicated and intellectually challenging than traditional negotiations. We will look at China and other Pacific Rim countries as examples of the challenges Americans face in negotiating across unfamiliar cultures.

In preparation for a presentation to the Milwaukee Trade Association, Cary did extensive research about negotiating on the Pacific Rim that included interviews with a number of Wisconsin-based executives who have conducted business in those countries. His research identified five barriers to reaching an agreement: structural, strategic, psychological, institutional, and cultural. We will address only the cultural barriers in this book, as they are the most relevant to incorporate into your approach and preparation for a negotiation.

The cultural barriers can be divided into five areas of differences:

- Communication styles
- Societal norms
- Worldviews
- Beliefs about what creates value
- Who legitimately makes decisions

The initial step in negotiating an international transaction successfully is to develop appropriate responses to cultural attitudes and expectations. Even though more Chinese companies are hiring English-speaking managers and engineers, you should seriously consider including a member of your team who speaks Chinese. This one step can prevent an unintentional loss of face and provide for more accurate communications. Saving face may be defined as the act of preserving one's prestige or dignity. China has a strong face-saving ethic, and negotiations may end if one party is caused to lose face. In China, saving face is more important than most business dealings.

At the foundation of Chinese negotiations is the promotion of *Li*, a long-term relationship, and *Quanxi*, the duty to maintain relationships. The Chinese need to be comfortable and trust the people they are dealing with. Their position in the negotiation is determined in advance, so if an impasse is encountered, typically they will need to withdraw and reach a new consensus.

China is a polychronic culture, that is, one where schedules are not quickly adhered to and time is seen as flexible. This is a potential "flashpoint," since American culture is monochronic—we tend to adhere to schedules more closely. In China, personal relationships take precedence over preset schedules, and schedules, even when built into a signed contract, remain approximate. American negotiations start when built into a contract and build to a relationship. This is called "building up." In contrast, the Chinese practice is "building down." They start with a relationship and build trust in order to reach an agreement. It usually requires more than three transactions to build the necessary level of trust with the Chinese. In this regard, the cultures of the parties are in opposition to each other.

In China, friendship implies obligation. In return for their friendship, the Chinese expect some concessions. It is best to perform small favors for the Chinese so they can reciprocate in the future.

Information exchange may be difficult at times, since the Chinese may withhold information to try to put you at a disadvantage. Their strategy may be to keep you off balance and defensive. You should strategically manage the exchange of information, make your expectations clear, and link the exchanges so you receive something of value in response for the information being shared.

Consensus decision-making is also a major part of the negotiating process in Korea, Japan, and Taiwan. This is the opposite of the American approach of empowerment of the team to make the deal. The consensus approach takes longer and negotiators should plan to spend at least 50 percent more time negotiating with Pacific Rim negotiators. Additionally, the final decision will be made at the upper level of their organization.

Below are some suggestions drawn from the interviews with Wisconsin businessmen and women who have negotiated with Pacific Rim companies:

1. Research the culture of the country in which you will negotiate.
2. Conduct a number of briefings with your executives prior to beginning the negotiation.
3. Formulate a list of dos and don'ts.
4. Select an experienced local agent to work with you.
5. Hire your own interpreter to reduce the potential for errors in translation.
6. Invest the time to develop a personal relationship with your negotiation counterpart.
7. Formalize your communications in writing and be clear in your requirements to avoid misunderstandings.
8. Show interest, not impatience; take a deep breath before you respond. Remember, you are building a long-term relationship.
9. Listen carefully and actively. Ask for clarification when necessary.
10. Control your emotions.

In summary, when negotiating internationally, you don't want to present as the "ugly American." Make sure you do your homework. The only way you can be successful is to familiarize yourself with the traditions, culture, and business practices of the country with which you will be negotiating.

Lessons Learned

- Gender can influence the outcome of a negotiation. Research shows that men and women approach, plan, and execute negotiations differently.

- Women, in general, are more concerned about building a relationship.

- Women are better "active listeners," while men are usually thinking of the next question to ask.

- Women are better advocates for others than for themselves.

- Assertive behavior in the workplace (on one's own behalf) is inconsistent with perceived female gender roles, so women may choose not to negotiate to avoid the threat of backlash from their supervisors and peers.

- When negotiations get "heated," women tend to withdraw while men tend to "dive in" and invest more energy into the negotiation.

- Women are more "collaborative" in their approach to a negotiation and work toward a creative and mutually satisfactory resolution.

- Men tend to be more "distributive" and to play the "zero-sum" game, where one person wins and the other loses.

- In the international business community we now live in, cross-cultural negotiations are the norm, not the exception. You need to arm yourself with knowledge of the country and culture in which you will be doing business and be prepared to conduct this negotiation differently from ones conducted in your hometown.

- Understand that in many Asian and Middle Eastern countries, the role women play in a business negotiation varies greatly. Failing to understand these cultural differences could negatively impact the results of your negotiation.

CHAPTER FOUR

Negotiating with Your Children

It's one in the morning and seven-month-old Jason is still crying in his crib. You just changed his diaper, rubbed him with baby lotion, and nursed him 'til he was satisfied. You want to pick him up and comfort him, but the pediatrician says you should let him cry himself to sleep. He has been crying for more than half an hour. You are getting angry and want to go back to sleep. You decide to go into his room and calm him by cradling him in your arms and singing him a lullaby until he falls asleep. Jason closes his eyes and begins to sleep. You put him down and leave the room. Again he begins to cry. Jason has learned his first negotiating behavior: he can manipulate his parents by crying.

Effective parenting is one of the most difficult tasks one will ever face. A great deal of parenting involves negotiating with one's offspring. Parenting lasts at least 20 years, and some say it never ends. Parents are "on call" 24/7. Parents receive no pay for their arduous work; in fact, it is quite costly to be a parent. The reward parents receive for a job well done is seeing that they have raised an independent, responsible young adult, and maybe also having some loving grandchildren.

The "Little Scientist" According to Jean Piaget

To better understand how to discuss/negotiate with young children, we must consider the theories of Jean Piaget, a well-known French developmental psychologist. Piaget noted that children were like "little scientists." They do many things randomly and then they note any interesting results. For example, the infant might kick his feet and in the process perhaps hit something that makes a sound. Subsequently the child exhibits the same kicking behavior purposely to continue eliciting that sound. This is how children learn to control their world. They learn that what they do has an effect.

According to Piaget, there are several factors in a child's cognitive development. He believed that the most critical one was the interactions with a child's peers. These interactions lead to cognitive conflicts, which turn into arguing and debating—an early application of negotiation (with their peers). This conflict requires the child to de-center himself and look at the other person's point of view. Piaget found that children are freer to confront ideas when working with peers compared to when they are talking to adults. Sometimes, though, children who work with other children at the same level of development tend not to argue. They, therefore, do not make the gains as they would make when confronted with conflict.

Piaget's studies revealed that children learn the basics of the art of negotiation early in their development. They are still not prepared to negotiate with an adult, but they will voice their opinion and should be heard. Shutting down any expression of their opinion early in development will impact their ability to express themselves in the future. Piaget helped demonstrate that childhood is a unique and important period of human development.

Since the child is born "naked and naïve," the child has no idea what is good/bad or normal/abnormal. It is up to the parent to establish the routines that the child is expected to follow. If, instead, the parent allows the child to set the routines, the child, who knows no better, is essentially "raising the parent." Classic examples are: allowing the toddler to frequently come into the parents' bedroom and disrupt their sleep, or allowing the child to substitute favorite foods for the meal provided. The parent must be the "foreman" for the first several years of the child's life.

When dealing with young children, parents should take a firm, directive approach. There is little negotiation during this period. Since the young child lives what she learns, the parent should not negotiate with her regarding basic routines such as bedtime, mealtime, or bath time. The child should be expected to follow the routine set by the parents. Knowing nothing else, the child will likely comply. If parents mistakenly begin negotiating with their young child regarding sleeping, eating, bathing, or toileting, from that point on, they will find that they are negotiating nearly everything with the child.

By the time the child is five or six, or even earlier, he can be allowed some choices. It is reasonable for the parent to give two choices for dessert, for example. At this age, many children begin to express their desires as to clothes to be worn, movies to be watched, and books to be read before bed. Again, the parent should not negotiate basic issues such as bedtime, personal grooming, and chores.

In setting expectations for behavior, parents must be explicit. The child must know and understand exactly what is expected of her and when the task is to be completed (as in the SMART goals, discussed earlier). It is often helpful to note specifically on a wall chart the specific tasks that the child is expected to perform. "Clean your room," "brush your teeth," "take a shower," "hang up your clothes," or "load the dishwasher" are examples of appropriate tasks that a child should complete, if the tasks are clearly stated. These chores give the child an opportunity to learn responsibility, be rewarded, and build self-esteem.

Communication Sins

Many parents unknowingly commit one or more of the following communication sins: monopolizing, lecturing and preaching, interrupting, dismissing, judging, and denying perceptions. We will discuss each of these "sins" and their negative impact on communications/negotiations with your child:

Monopolizing. Communication research has indicated that when conversing with their children, parents monopolize upward of 90 percent of the conversation. A typical conversation consists of the parent making a point at great length, interspersed with the parent asking the child a number of questions. These questions are "closed ended" and require a "yes" or "no" answer; they do not encourage an exchange of information. Usually this type of one-sided interaction continues for up to thirty minutes at a time. It's no wonder that kids often complain they "can't talk to" their parents and that their parents don't understand them.

To avoid monopolizing, parents must pay attention to the ratio of their speaking time to that of their child. For you to effectively communicate with your child, especially when he reaches the teenage years, he should be able to speak about half the time. To engage in an effective communication you need to ask "open-ended" questions, questions that can be answered in phrases or sentences and usually elicit a more extensive response. Some examples of these types of questions are:

- What do you think about . . . ?
- How do you feel about . . . ?
- What is your opinion about . . . ?
- Why is it important that . . . ?
- When do you think would be a good time for you to return from the movie?

In order to obtain additional information, parents can use the following "follow-up" questions or statements:

- That's interesting, please tell me more.
- Why is this so important to you?

Lecturing and preaching. This concept is closely related to monopolizing in that the parent over-controls the conversation and does most of the talking. In addition to monopolizing the conversation, the parent takes on a moralistic tone and often lectures at great length. More than likely this is not the first time the child has heard this lecture. When parents lecture, a telltale glaze usually comes over the adolescent's eyes; at this point, only the parents are listening—to themselves.

Preaching is lecturing with morals. It often begins with the parent saying, "When I was your age . . . ," and then the parent rambles on for fifteen minutes or more. Many adolescents believe their parents were "born old" or are dumb when it comes to understanding their own situations. Preaching deteriorates the communication process and is not an effective way to teach values. It is a "one-way" communication process and does not permit the child or teen to engage in a dialogue with her parents. Remember how many of us fell asleep in our church or synagogue listening to a lengthy sermon from our priest, minister, or rabbi? You have that same impact on your child when you preach.

Interrupting. When participating in a negotiation or a discussion, you need to let the other party state his intent or position without being interrupted. Here is your opportunity to gather information, or understand his point of view. When you interrupt, you break your child's "chain of thought," and show disrespect. As was mentioned in an earlier chapter, you want to build trust in the relationship, and interrupting does the opposite. In fact, it angers people when they cannot complete a thought. Interrupting elevates the level of stress in the communication process and may even destroy the process altogether.

If your intent is to gather information, show the proper respect and listen carefully to your child. If you require clarification of any statement, use the "active listening" tool discussed in Chapter Two and paraphrase when he finishes speaking. Your goal is to facilitate communication and gather the information you need to make a decision or influence your child's or adolescent's behavior in a positive manner. Don't lose sight of your goal or let your emotion drive the conversation.

Dismissing feelings. When discussing feelings with your child or teenager, don't dismiss her perception of the situation. As an example, Sue says to her mom, "I'm so mad at Aunt Louise for what she said. I hate her!" Mom responds, "You don't mean that. Aunt Louise likes you. You are her favorite niece. I don't want to hear you talk like that anymore!" What the mother did here is dismiss the validity of her child's perceptions and demonstrate she was not listening. This shuts down communication and diminishes the level of trust.

One strategy you may elect to use in such a situation is to openly state your feelings regarding a situation, a process, or a point made. As a parent, you may state, "I am uncomfortable with the way you are talking about your aunt." And pose the question, "Why do you feel that way towards her?" You are now using an open-ended question to elicit information about your child's feelings without dismissing them. This will build trust and the relationship, while maintaining an open communication channel.

Judging. A basic tenet of psychotherapy is that the therapist should not make value judgments about her client. This is especially true about the client's feelings or attitudes. To a large degree, parents should follow the same rule. One way to extinguish a communication or shut down a negotiation is to make a "value judgment" about the other person's feelings, values, attitudes, or statements. As a parent, you want to teach your children to feel comfortable with communicating with you, so reserve judgment.

Denying perceptions. If you want your children to share their perceptions, it is best not to deny what they perceive or view. All people are entitled to their own perceptions. Communicating with your children that what they are thinking or feeling is wrong will shut down the flow of communications. The real risk is that they will begin to doubt their own perceptions.

When negotiating, you don't want to deny someone's perception, you want them to explain "why" they see it that way. This is an opportunity for you to gather additional information that could aid you in successfully completing the negotiation. It has been found when people explain their feelings or perceptions, they sometimes realize that their perceptions are incorrect and are open to adjusting them. A number of listening strategies to facilitate communication with your adolescent are included in the next section.

Facilitating Communication

Parents should develop some of the counseling techniques used by therapists to foster better communication with their teens; one of them is reflective listening. By using reflective listening, you don't commit any of the sins of communications discussed above. The reflective listener remains quiet, calm, and interested, and virtually becomes a "mirror." For example: An adolescent girl is depressed over breaking up with her boyfriend. She states, "Mom I loved him! What am I going to do?" The mother responds properly, "You seem really sad. Tell me more about it." The teen replies, "We have been arguing for the past weeks, but I didn't think it would lead to this."

In this example, the mother did not commit any of the sins of communication. Instead, she used the following tools: she listened; she paraphrased, and asked for more information. Her daughter felt that she was heard, recognized that her mother heard her, and was encouraged to continue expressing herself openly without being judged.

Cueing

Every person experienced with dealing with children knows that it is important to cue children every time there is a "change of set," that is, a change in the situation. For example, Larry's wife, Nan, taught fourth grade for nearly thirty years, and whenever her students were about to move from the classroom to the playground, she would remind them what their playground behavior was supposed to "look like." If the children were moving from the classroom to the lunchroom, again, she would clearly and explicitly remind the children how they were to behave. Also, if the children were moving from the classroom to the bus, she would remind them what proper bus behavior is. It is most effective in working with children to remind them specifically and explicitly what their behavior is expected to look like when they move from one activity to another or from one setting to another. Behavior that may be appropriate at home, for example, may not be appropriate at a restaurant or at a relative's house. Children respond positively to clearly defined expected behaviors.

Negotiating with the Pre-adolescent

As the child matures into preadolescence, she becomes very familiar with her basic chores. Little, if any, direction should be necessary. More complex chores, such as doing the laundry or helping with the yardwork, should be added to the chore list as the child matures. Remember, as an adult, you should demonstrate the expected behaviors to ensure the potential for success.

Pre-adolescents must be allowed to make more of their own decisions. This is where the true negotiation occurs between parent and child. At this time, the primary role of the parent is to briefly and succinctly, and without any hysteria, point out to the teen the tasks she has and what may be the consequences of her choices. For example, if the child says she refuses to do her math assignment tonight, it is not the duty of the parent to *force* the child to do it. Doing so will certainly be unpleasant; it will strain the parent-child relationship, and it will not lead to scholarship. Instead, the parent should calmly inform the child that if she chooses to ignore the homework, her teacher will apply an appropriate consequence. This consequence may range from having to do the assignment during recess for less credit to receiving a detention. If the child continues to make such a negative choice, she might be faced with retention in the grade. In this manner, she is allowed to make a choice and is allowed to face the natural/logical consequences of her decision. This approach prepares the child for life, because this is how the real world works. If you are late for work too many times, the boss doesn't call you in the morning to wake you up, he simply fires you.

Lessons Learned

- Studies by Piaget revealed that children learn early in their development the basics of the art of negotiation. They are still not prepared to negotiate with an adult, but they will voice their opinion and should be heard.

- If parents mistakenly begin negotiating with their young child regarding sleeping, eating, or toileting, from that point on, they will find that they are negotiating nearly everything with the child. Children must learn early on that some topics and situations are "non-negotiable."

- In the early stages of children's development, you have the opportunity to teach them about the consequences of their behavior. Children should be informed by the parents that not doing an assigned task or homework will result in some negative consequence, for example, lost privileges at home or detention at school.

- While communicating with their children, parents should be aware of the downsides of monopolizing, interrupting, lecturing, dismissing, and denying their children's perceptions. You do not want to commit these communication sins, as they will lessen the impact of your communication with your child.

- Parents should practice "reflective listening" to demonstrate that they are listening and interested in what their child is saying.

- It is most effective in working with children to remind them specifically and explicitly what their behavior is expected to look like when they move from one activity to another. Children respond positively to expected behaviors that are clearly defined.

Chapter Five

Dealing Positively with
Your Adolescent Children

Lisa has invited her friends to come over for the afternoon. Her mother sees that her room looks like a tornado had just passed through. Lisa's bed is not made, and her clothes are thrown all over the floor. Her mother confronts Lisa, telling her that she cannot have her friends over until the room is cleaned. Lisa begins to pout and says that her mother always picks on her and favors her younger brother. Lisa has just changed the conversation so as not to address the real issue. Her mother refocuses the conversation on Lisa's messy room and restates that she cannot have guests until the room is clean; her mother clearly states that it is "non-negotiable."

Many parents continue to raise their teen as they did when the teen was half her current age. This simply does not work. It is entirely appropriate to be firmly directive with a seven- or eight-year-old, but it will not sit well with an adolescent. Parents of a teen must graduate from the role of "foreman" to "consultant," and even to "mediator." The "consultant" lays out the choices and the likely consequences, but the teen makes the final decision and accepts the consequences of her choice. When parents assume the role of the "mediator," they are attempting to help facilitate a solution to a problem between siblings, relatives, or friends. This chapter suggests strategies for dealing with the small number of "non-negotiables" that will consume much of your parenting time.

Communication and Negotiation with Your Teen

Teens universally complain that their parents "don't listen." Conversely, many parents struggle with conversing and negotiating with their adolescents. Attempts at communication often result in yelling, doors being slammed, feelings of resentment, and a sense of hopelessness about the possible resolution of issues. Be aware that teens sometimes try to use a strategy of "divide and conquer." They appeal one parent's decision to the other parent in the hope of gaining support for their argument. Parents need to stay united in their decisions, otherwise the teen will play one parent against the other.

Often when a parent approaches a teen, it is to complain or scold him. The teen soon learns that when their parent wants to speak with him, it likely means he is in trouble. Effective communication or negotiation is not about to be successful under these conditions. Parents must be as diligent in noting positive behaviors in their teen as they are at reporting the undesirable acts they observe. As mentioned earlier, "anchoring" a communication with a positive behavior prior to referencing a negative one keeps the other person open to what is being communicated.

All too often parents' discussions with their teens become long-winded lectures. A one-way conversation does not promote communication or negotiation and, again, teaches the teen that speaking with his parents is unpleasant. Parents should allow their teen to speak, at least as much as the parent does, and encourage the teen to talk by again using open-ended questions such as, "What do you think about . . . ?" This is a perfect opportunity to apply the strategies of "active listening" discussed in earlier chapters. These strategies will demonstrate that you are listening and interested in what your teen is saying.

Limit preaching and attempts to persuade. Since parents are older and (hopefully) wiser, they tend to preach to their kids. This is understandable, as no parent wants his child to fail, or to repeat the mistakes that the parent remembers making. However, most teens view their parents as old and out of touch, so the "sermons" are not well received. Parents should recall their own adolescence and how unwilling they were to accept their parents' advice. By the same token, attempting to argue with or persuade a teen is wasteful and painful. It is most unlikely that a parent preaches to or argues a point with the teen, and the teen responds, "Mom/Dad thanks for bringing that up. I'll do exactly as you said." Parents have the right and the duty to briefly make their position known, but, in most cases, the teen should be allowed to make a choice. It can often be helpful to offer a few choices, especially with younger teens. Teens learn best when the "world" applies a consequence to their actions, not when the parent applies punishment. We learn more from our failures than our successes.

Don't match your teen's emotion. Adolescents are naturally labile, that is, moody. Don't let the teen control the tone of the home. In some homes, parents can only be as happy as the saddest teen in the house. If the teen is "losing it," it does not mean the parent has to "lose it" too. Remember, "Misery loves company." Make your point briefly and walk away. If the emotional level is too high, it may be better to withdraw, take a break, and set another time for the discussion.

Allow teens to learn to take responsibility for their behavior and their decisions. Larry often tells parents, "If teens are *forced* to be responsible, they're not!" Adolescents, just as most adults, learn best from the consequences of their acts. Larry has seen dozens of young adults in his career who earned decent grades in high school only because their parents forced them to do their homework or to study for a test by threating some kind of punishment if they didn't.

Unfortunately, many of these students then proceeded to drop out of college because no one was making them study. Responsible behavior is learned—not coerced.

Teens also need to be involved in determining their punishment for violating an agreement or rule. It is critical that they understand that there are repercussions for bad decisions. One weekend when Cary and his wife, Susie, were going away for the day, their teenage daughter asked if she could go to the Six Flags amusement park with a friend. They said "no" because they felt that this friend was not a responsible individual. When they came home, their daughter was sunburned, and they asked if she went to Six Flags with her friend. She said yes. Cary and Susie stated she was to be grounded for a weekend evening for ignoring their directions. They gave her the opportunity to select the weekend night that she would be grounded. She selected that Friday night.

On Friday, her best friend called and invited her to join her family at a fish fry dinner. She asked, "Can I go?" and Cary and Susie said no. They reiterated that she had selected to be grounded that night. She requested to change the grounding to Saturday night, and they again said, "no." She called her friend back and said that "they would not let her go." She saw her parents as the bad guys by not relenting. However, she learned the appropriate lesson from this experience.

Negotiate over money and other resources. In many instances, teens ask for an advance in their allowance or a loan to purchase items such as clothing, to download music, or to go to the movies. In these cases, there is an opportunity to negotiate and link the loan or advance to a behavioral change or the performance of a task. For example, "Clean up the garage, and I will extend you a loan." Or, "Maintain a B average for this quarter, and I will pay for your flying lessons." The latter deal worked with Cary's teenaged son while he was in high school. One quarter his grades dropped, and he was "grounded" for the next quarter until his grades improved. He learned "a deal is a deal" and there are penalties to be paid for non-performance. Never again did his grades drop below the required B level during his high school career. Saying and doing are two different things; when parents follow through on their promises, they gain credibility in the eyes of their teen.

Another example involving Cary's son took place when he was in college. During the summer vacation, he was working as a flight instructor at a local private airfield and wanted to achieve his multi-engine rating. He said he needed $2,500 to pay for the plane rental and fuel. Since Cary had financed his earlier ratings, he figured Dad would underwrite this next rating. He was mistaken; it was time for another "life lesson." Even though Cary had the needed funds, he told his son he needed to develop another solution. His son openly expressed his disappointment and left the room, frustrated. A number of days later, Cary's son came back and said that he got one of his students to agree to let him use his twin engine plane in exchange for private instrument lessons, if Cary would pay for the fuel. Since he had negotiated the use of the plane, an option Cary had not considered, Cary agreed to underwrite the cost of the fuel. It turned out to be a win-win for both parties and a lesson well learned. Don't enter into a negotiation without developing one or more optional solutions (BATNA) to the problem.

Avoid judging and dismissing feelings. Nobody appreciates it when someone judges them or dismisses their feelings. Parents must realize that teens are in the awkward stage of struggling to find their personal identity at the same time they want to be accepted by their peers, not parents. Telling teens they are forbidden to associate with a peer because you view that peer as an outcast and how they dress makes them look like an idiot, or that the intense emotion they have about somebody they are dating is "just puppy love" will not facilitate communication with your adolescent. If you believe you need to comment, preface your brief statement with something like "It seems to me . . . ." Again, here is another opportunity to introduce the active listening tools mentioned earlier.

Listen. Listening actively or responsively means more than just being quiet. It involves not interrupting and not monopolizing the conversation. Active listening involves maintaining eye contact, smiling and nodding appropriately, and asking for more information, such as "Tell me more about that" and "Why do you feel so strongly about that?"

Paraphrase as a cornerstone of communication. Paraphrasing involves actively listening. Once the parent has heard what the teen has to say on a topic, the parent first summarizes the teen's major points to complete the communication and facilitate the negotiation. It might be helpful for the parent to take notes so that the teen believes that his comments are being noted and the parent remembers them all when paraphrasing. The parents are demonstrating they feel their teen's points are important and possibly valid. Ideally the teen would be taking notes as his parent speaks as well.

When the teen makes a request, the parent should ask her to review all her reasons. The parent should listen actively and responsively, and when it appears that the teen has finished, ask if she has anything to add. When she acknowledges that she has made every point she can think of, then the parent can summarize all the points and ask for confirmation. When the teen confirms that the parent has accurately reviewed all of the issues, the parent can then provide a response, positive or negative, and the discussion is closed. This procedure does not guarantee the teen will be pleased, but it does ensure that she will not be able to say her parent never listened. This strategy will also maximize the chance of ongoing parent-teen communication and negotiation.

Parents should not feel that they have to immediately respond to a teen's request for permission to do something. Teens typically want what they want when they want it and often will pressure a parent for an immediate answer to something that can wait. Consider responding with, "I'll speak with Mom/Dad and we'll get back to you after dinner." This strategy permits a parent to think about the request, consult the other parent, and also to have this important conversation at a time and place that might be more conducive to a discussion.

The Allowance: A Strategy for Teaching the Value of Money

There should be a systematic relationship between the money allotted and the tasks performed. Parents should clearly and specifically outline the chores/tasks they wish to have performed by the teen and assign a value. There should be deadlines for the completion of each task and clear instructions on how the task should be performed. Timelines and the level of compensation can be negotiated, but, as always, some aspects of the negotiation are non-negotiable. In the real world, deadlines need to be met or there are repercussions.

For example, if you want to have your car detailed by your teen, you should specify what to do, how you want it done, and how much you will pay. You must explain in detail your expectations for the outcome of the task in detail. Your negotiation over price should include specific tasks to be performed, i.e., wash the exterior, wipe down the interior with a fabric or leather cleaner, clean the interior glass, vacuum and shampoo the carpets, and polish the wheel covers and tires. What you pay for this service should be based on what it would cost if a detailer did it, less any supplies you need to provide for the task.

Connecting specific tasks to specific amounts of compensation is a most effective way to motivate your teen to complete the assigned tasks. This is an early life lesson for teens in the value of their labors. If the teen does not complete the task as outlined, then the monetary value placed on the task will be reduced. The teen should be paid for the portions of the task completed. He should be reminded that during the negotiation about compensation the tasks were clearly outlined and that he was expected to complete the entire assignment. Our observations reinforce the thesis that teens will learn from their mistakes and will adjust their future behavior accordingly.

The Curfew

The curfew is something that all teens and young adults feel is negotiable. It is not unusual for adolescents to attempt to extend their curfew by using various arguments and rationalizations. Parents can respond by saying, "We love you and worry about you." You can also use "information power" by informing the teen that most serious vehicle accidents occur after the bars close. You may also use your "legitimate power," that is, the perceived power you have as a parent. The following example demonstrates how with "active listening" and "legitimate power," Larry was able to convince his son that his request for an extension in curfew was not reasonable.

When Larry's son was seventeen, he came to his father asking if he and a friend could go to a concert on a Wednesday evening and stay out quite late. Larry asked his son to explain fully what his intent was. He proceeded to tell his father that the group he wanted to see, The Smashing Pumpkins, was one of his favorite groups, and that he probably would not be able to see them again for a long time. He promised he would do his homework before he left for the concert. He noted the concert would probably run until approximately 2 a.m., but he assured Larry that he would awaken Thursday morning to get to school on time.

After his son was allowed to fully explain his position, Larry repeated his position back to his son by paraphrasing his original statement. "The Smashing Pumpkins are one of your favorite groups; you may not get a chance to see them again live for quite some time; you will complete your homework before leaving for the concert; and you will awaken on time Thursday morning to get to school."

When Larry used "active listening" to repeat his position, his son acknowledged that Larry had completely and correctly heard his argument. Larry then informed his son that while he appreciated his son's position, as a responsible parent, he could not allow him to stay out until 2 a.m. on a school night. Besides, the city's curfew ruling would also prevent that from happening. His son indicated he was unhappy with Larry's answer, but was not surprised by it, and walked off. While his son was not pleased, one thing he certainly could not say was that his father did not hear him. Many times when you permit your young adult to explain their position on a situation, they realize that their argument is not supportable. In this example, Larry used "legitimate power" (the city curfew ruling) as a reason for not granting his son's request.

Here is another example of the dreaded curfew: Cary's daughter was 16 and had an eleven o'clock curfew. At 10:45, she called and said that she "was having fun at the party and wanted to stay till midnight." Cary responded that they had an agreed-upon curfew, it was "non-negotiable," and he expected his daughter to be home by eleven. He hung up, and ten minutes later he heard a car come to a quick stop in the driveway, its breaks squealing. His daughter entered the house and slammed the front door. Then she slammed her bedroom door. His wife Susie said, "Go speak with her." Cary replied, "I will handle it in the morning," and he went to sleep.

The next morning his daughter showed up at breakfast with a frown on her face. She complained that Cary had embarrassed her in front of her friends. Cary responded that we had a deal, and "I don't renegotiate a deal at the last minute."

By the time the family sat down at breakfast, the level of emotion had been reduced and they could talk as adults without anger interfering with the conversation. As a result of the discussion, Cary's daughter learned that if she wanted an extension on a curfew, she had to call earlier in the evening, not right before the curfew takes effect.

The Dating Game, Hanging Out, and Other Social Interactions

Parents often struggle with the question of when their daughter or son should begin to date. There are many factors to consider when your child requests permission to date. In many cases, adolescents begin to date before their parents are aware they are in a relationship. It is not uncommon for young teens to meet up in groups at the local mall and pair up with their "special" friend. Unless someone sees your child holding hands or kissing and informs you, you may not know your child is in a relationship.

Your goal should be to create an open and safe dialogue so your teen will not be afraid to come to you with her concerns and fears.

With the advent of cellular phones, these adolescents are "FaceTiming" and texting each other from their bedrooms. In some cases, they are sending each other provocative selfies—"sexting." Teens must understand that their phones are not private and parents may check their phone at any time. Any misuse of the cell phone, such as going to inappropriate sites or sexting, will result in the loss of access to their cell phone.

It is up to you, the parent, to put guidelines in place before your child begins to "hang out" with friends at the mall or other meeting place. Most malls have posted rules of conduct at each entrance, and some state that minor children must be accompanied by an adult.

We suggest that you:

- Make your child aware of the rules of conduct posted at the mall.
- Set guidelines for the use of their cell phones.
- Explain how a person's privacy can be compromised when sharing selfies, photos, and videos. Your child needs to understand that once something is transmitted, it is always available online and easily accessible to others.
- Make sure your child realizes that many of your rules are "non-negotiable" and for her safety.
- As part of your discussion/negotiation, agree on time limits and acceptable behaviors when they are with friends in the mall, on dates, or at the movies.
- Be prepared to make some concessions during your discussion/negotiation, but link your concession to something you desire on your child's part. An example would be additional time with friends exchanged for maintaining her room or performing other chores around the house.

There is no doubt you will receive pushback from your teen. You will hear, "You are unfair, no one else's mom makes her kid do that," etc. Your response should be a positive statement, "I am trying to keep you safe because I love you."

As your teen gets more mature, you can sit down and negotiate over who can be in his car and how late he can be out on a date. As teens, both Cary and Larry heard this phrase many times: "I want you home by 11:00 p.m." As a parent, you need to be consistent in your enforcement of curfews, especially if you have several teenagers. Curfews will change as the teen matures and demonstrates responsible behaviors.

The Family Car

Over the years, we have heard numerous stories about conflicts over the use of the family car. In today's world, the typical middle class family has one or more cars, and teenagers often earn the right to drive them.

Knowing that your teenager will ultimately get a driver's license and will want to use the car, you need to begin to discuss the ground rules for use of the family vehicle prior to the acquisition of her learner's permit. This is a negotiation where you are in the "driver's seat" and not a passenger. Don't give up this advantage. You need to go into this negotiation with a list of your expectations for your teen's behavior when asking for the use of the car and when operating it. Remember that driving is a privilege and it has to be earned. It comes with responsibilities and accountabilities.

A common conflict arises when the teen advises his parents, "I have a date. I need the car tonight." The issue is that you were never told in advance that the car would be needed, and you may have plans that require the car. One way to avoid these potential conflicts is to have a schedule for the use of the car and rules for its use. Possibly you could limit the teen to one night each weekend.

Here are some additional rules to be considered:

1. Who can be with your teen when she drives? Many states have specific laws regarding when teenagers can drive and who can or must be with them.

2. The curfew.

3. Where they can go.

4. The number of people in the car. A study performed by the American Medical Association reported that the number of accidents increased

dramatically as the number of other teens in the car increased. These and other studies have led some states to restrict the number of teens in a car at any one time.

So the open questions are: what do you need to negotiate regarding your teen driving and how do you go about it? Because there are laws that govern teen driving in some states, there is no need to negotiate these rules; you simply need to reinforce them with your teen. This is a positive use of legitimate power. That said, most of the important negotiating levers parents have with the family car are at parental discretion and should be considered as tools to promote your teen's well-being. Below are some of the potential negotiating tools you can use that are associated with the family car.

You will need to spell out your expectations regarding the following: fuel replacement, vehicle maintenance, and keeping the interior clean and the exterior washed. If you provide the vehicle with a full tank, then you may want it back with a full tank. Some of our friends have complained that they started to drive to work and had to stop for gas because their teen did not replace the fuel used—and they arrived late for work.

You could also elect to tie the use of the car to the maintenance of grades or the completion of assigned tasks, such as mowing the lawn, raking the leaves, washing the dishes, or ferrying their younger siblings to play dates, music lessons, or other activities. Teens want to drive and will even accept the responsibility of transporting their younger sister or brother in order to get driving time.

Other elements that could be negotiated include your teen's contribution to the additional cost of insurance, vehicle maintenance, and repairs. According to published insurance industry statistics, there will be a fender bender in your teen's future, and you need to stress that he will share in any cost related to the repair. Since teen drivers have a high accident rate, this is more of a reality than they realize.

With all this discussion of expenses, actual and potential, the money needs to come from somewhere. It should not be from you, the parent. Teens need to earn their way. A part-time job should be acquired to teach responsibility and also to provide the cash flow needed to pay for the gas, oil, and related expenses. Parents have the option to cover these expenses if the teen is engaged in some worthy activity, such as athletics, band, drama, or volunteer work.

Too many parents completely underwrite the expense of driving, and the teen is not accountable for any expenses related to the use of the car. That is an error and a missed learning opportunity. In the negotiation, you need to be ready to state that if her grades drop or she fails to keep the vehicle fueled, there will be repercussions. You should not be vague—you need to be specific. You need to state that she will lose the use of the vehicle for a specific period of time: a weekend, a week, or more. If she has a part-time job, during this "time out," you may need to drive and pick her up from work. The lessons learned are far more important than the inconvenience to your schedule.

When Cary's son started driving the family vehicle, he drove it to flying lessons on Sunday mornings. He also used it for occasional dates on Friday and Saturday nights. One night after he dropped Cary off at a local college to teach his graduate class, his son was clocked speeding on a street near their house. The officer who stopped him had a son in the local Boy Scout Troop where Cary was the scoutmaster. The officer elected to give Cary's son a warning. The next day Cary received a phone call informing him of the warning. Cary told "lead foot" that the next time that happened, he would take away the keys. Cary's son got the message and eased up on the gas.

When Larry's son was sixteen and had earned his driver's license, the rule was only one passenger in the car—to reduce distractions and liability with an inexperienced driver. One evening, while returning home from work, Larry noted his son's car ahead. Larry sped up to say hello. At the stoplight, Larry noted there was not one passenger in the son's compact car—there were four! Larry stated: "Home!!" By the time his son got home, Larry was awaiting him with a steering wheel lock, which was immediately applied—to remain for a week. His son asked how was supposed to take his friends home and get to school, etc., to which Larry said his son needed to work that out and follow the rules of car use.

You need to stay consistent with your expectations and discipline in order for them to be effective. Teens are constantly testing the limits and boundaries. It is expected behavior within that age group. You may bend but must not break.

Buying a Car

Most teenagers want to have their own car. If you are hearing this request over and over again from your teenager and it is something that you think you might consider, we suggest that you wait until your adolescent has responsibly driven your family car for more than a year before letting him have a car of his own. Many parents prefer to purchase a used car rather than a new vehicle. The parent has to consider a number of things, including the model, the size, the horsepower, and the price. If the parents are buying the car, these decisions are made by the parents, with input from their teen. If the purchase is being made by the adolescent, he should have a greater amount of input, but this should be tempered by the parent.

Another consideration when purchasing a car is insurance. Rates will depend on the age of the vehicle, its type (sedan, SUV, convertible, compact, luxury, etc.) the horsepower, and the experience of the driver. As noted previously, the accident rate for teen drivers is much higher than for older drivers.

Thus it may be in your best interest to have an umbrella policy in addition to your liability coverage to better protect your home and other assets.

In some instances, parents may decide to buy a new car for themselves and have their teen inherit their vehicle. Alternatively, parents may decide to buy a safe, sensible vehicle for their son or daughter. This may require some negotiation, because the teen may want something that is fun, fancy, and fast. Having their own car is the key to freedom of movement for teens.

Buying a vehicle is an opportunity for two separate negotiations, one with the dealer or seller and the other with the driver. Let's look at the negotiation with the driver first, because until you can agree as to the type, size, and style of the vehicle, you cannot begin your search.

Parents and their teen both need to be deeply involved in the selection and purchase of the teen's first vehicle. Even if your teen is paying for the vehicle with his own savings, parental input in the selection is critical. Show your teen how to gather the data on the vehicle he wishes to drive. The parents and their teen should work together to establish a set of decision criteria for the purchase. Examples of decision criteria are: price, safety rating, engine size and fuel economy, maintenance history, and cost of insuring the vehicle.

As mentioned earlier, the accident rate is highest among teenage drivers, so safety is a major consideration. In choosing a vehicle, you would want to use "information power" to convince your child that the vehicles you are suggesting are safe, will incur reasonable insurance rates, and will be in the proper price range.

This information can be derived from the following sources:

- The *Kelly Blue Book* [www.kbb.com]
- *Consumer Reports* [www.consumerreports.org]
- National Transportation Safety Board (NTSB) [www.Safercar.gov]
- Your insurance agent

The *Kelly Blue Book* provides the retail prices on vehicles you are considering. *Consumer Reports* independently rates the various models with regard to safety and reliability, and publishes consumer comments. The NTSB will provide safety ratings for each vehicle you are contemplating.

Your insurance agent will provide the collision and liability rates for any of the vehicles you are considering. Add this to any financing for the vehicle, and you will have your total monthly expenses, less gas, oil, and maintenance.

Once you have assembled all the information you need, review it with your teen. Prior to this meeting, it is suggested that you invite your teen to independently collect information that supports his choice. As information is shared, common ground is revealed; this builds toward a consensus and a resolution of the issue or issues being negotiated.

Prior to the negotiation, you should review the ground rules for the negotiation/discussion. These ground rules would include: Who goes first, no interruptions, no loud voices (show respect), no threats, and the ability to "agree to disagree." Let your teen go first and present his case. Be sure not to interrupt his presentation and take notes as he presents his case. When he finishes, practice "active listening" and restate his main points in your own words in order to demonstrate that you heard and understood him. Where you are unsure, ask for clarification. Be sure you let him know how you are impacted by what he said. Use descriptive phrases such as:

- I am *concerned* about your ability to afford your choice of vehicle.
- The level of safety of the chosen vehicle *concerns* us.
- I feel *uncomfortable* with your choice of vehicle.
- Help me *understand* why you selected this particular vehicle.

These statements will communicate to your teen that you feel there are some questions that still need to be addressed. These "open-ended" questions require a factual response and not a simple yes or no answer. Once you have narrowed the choices using the agreed-upon criteria, you can begin to search the Internet for available vehicles that meet those criteria.

Getting a Tattoo or Piercings

If you haven't already noticed, many of today's young adults, both men and women, have colorful and intricate tattoos on various locations on their bodies. Many have "sleeves" that run from their shoulder to their hand. Others have large tattoos on their lower back, often called "tramp stamps." These tattoos are no longer limited to bikers, Hollywood types, sailors, servicemen, and rock musicians. Some young adults cover themselves with "ink," or "body art," and use multiple body piercings as a way to make a statement about their individuality. In some cases, they get tattoos to fit in with their peers.

When discussing/negotiating tattoos and body piercings with your teen, you need to arm her with information in order to influence her decision. It is critical to share the fact with your young adult that this "body art" and these piercings are permanent. Yes, they can be removed and repaired, but that process is time consuming, very expensive, and quite painful.

When one of the Larry's sons became an adolescent and then a young adult, Larry tried his best to counsel him against getting a tattoo, as they were becoming popular among young people at that time. One of the thoughts Larry shared with his sons, that he believed worked fairly well, was this statement: "Whenever you go into a bar, look for a woman who is wearing a tattoo. You now know that she is capable of making a decision that she is likely to be sorry for later." Larry believed that this politically incorrect statement had the desired effect, since neither of his sons has gotten a tattoo.

Lessons Learned

- There is nothing wrong with using the term "non-negotiable" when having a discussion with your adolescent. He is still your child who is living in your home; he needs to respect your wishes and standards of behavior.

- Listen actively and speak concretely. When giving directions, making requests, reinforcing, or even scolding your teen, you must be clear, concise, and specific. We suggest that you engage your teen in "active listening" and request he review what you just communicated.

- Be sure to use "active listening" techniques to clarify information and demonstrate that you are concerned about what your teen is communicating.

- Use "open-ended" questions during your discussions with your teen in order to gather additional information. Questions that can be answered with "yes" or "no" provide little useable information.

- Create an open and safe dialogue so your teen will not be afraid to come to you with her concerns and fears. Don't be afraid to discuss dating with your teen early on; express your concerns regarding intimacy, encouraging sensible and safe behaviors.

- In order to maintain a high level of trust in the relationship, follow through on your promises and articulate that you expect the other party to do the same.

- Discuss the establishment and enforcement of ground rules regarding behavior, use of the family vehicles, and other family responsibilities. Remember to stress your concern for your teen's safety in regard to operating the family vehicles.

- Don't let your teen "divide and conquer." Also, be careful of implying that you are okay with the issue before you consult with your partner, because if the answer ultimately becomes "no," you have inadvertently painted your partner as the "bad guy."

- Use "We'll get back to you." Teens typically want what they want when they want it. Often the teen will pressure the parent for an immediate answer to something that can wait. Consider responding with, "I'll speak with Mom/Dad and we'll get back to you after dinner." This strategy will permit the important conversation to take place at a time and place that is more conducive to a discussion.

(continued)

- When making important decisions, for example buying a car for your teen, make sure you have developed the necessary "decision criteria" with his assistance. In this way, he is part of the process and will better support the final decision.

- During many negotiations, as information is shared, common ground is revealed, which builds toward a consensus and a resolution of the issue or issues being negotiated. Be open to unexpected solutions that fully accomplish your goals.

Chapter Six

Negotiating with Your Boomerang Child

Adam has just graduated from college with a degree in business. While celebrating with his family and friends at dinner, Adam informs his parents that even though he has a job, he needs to move back home. He wants to pay off his student loans and cannot afford to pay rent or furnish an apartment. One problem is that his parents have already engaged an interior decorator to convert his room into a den. If they agree to let Adam move back into their home, they need to negotiate two things, a "move-out-by" date and appropriate house rules for their son. This could be a very contentious discussion.

After your adult children leave the household and proceed on their educational journey or pursue other interests, their relationship with you continues to evolve. While at college, they are subject to the institution's rules and standards of behavior. No longer are they under your roof and subject to your rules. The topics you tend to negotiate are their monthly finances; how often they "check in" by phone, email, or text; and the frequency of visitation. That scenario changes if they request to move back to your home after they complete their degree.

Moving Back Home

In the twenty-first century, a new phenomenon has arisen, the "new normal" for our young adults. Even if they have gainful employment, males and females are moving back into their parents' homes after graduation from college or graduate school. According to a recent *Wall Street Journal* article titled "Congratulations to Class of 2014, Most Indebted Ever," the average college graduate owes $33,000 in college loans, and the amount is increasing every year. Upwards of 70 percent of undergraduates with bachelor's degrees are leaving schools with student loans. A recent survey of college seniors found that 85 percent expect to return home after graduation. Why most grads move back is simple: most entry-level positions do not pay a salary sufficient to cover their living expenses and the cost of paying back their college loans. Until they reach a level of salary that covers both living expenses and loan repayment, they need to move back home.

In some cases, recent grads move back because they don't have a job. You love your children, but they need to be independent and have their privacy—as do you. Parents fear that their adult children will use a difficult economy to justify an incomplete job search. What options do you have? In the balance of this chapter, we will explore a number of options put forth in a 2013 article by Rand Spero "Adult Children Moving Back Home: The Boomerang Generation and the New Normal," published by the Clay Center for Young Healthy Minds. These options can provide a roadmap that permits the returning young adult to gain his independence and you to maintain your privacy without negatively impacting the parent-child relationship.

The Appropriate Rules

Once back under your roof, these young adults who have led an independent lifestyle for four to six years are now again subject to your house rules. This can be a source of great conflict between returning graduates and their parents and also with their younger siblings. As young adults, they are dating, often sexually active, and very social, which means they need their privacy and will probably keep inconsistent schedules. This can disrupt family dinners, study schedules, and other family activities.

It is extremely important that ground rules be established prior to the young adult returning home. In many cases, the parents have already reassigned their adult child's room to another sibling or even repurposed it as a den, sewing room, or guest room. In rare cases, a surviving grandparent has moved in and taken over the room. A returning child will in some instances create a three-generation home.

In addition to setting a time limit on how long your adult child will live at home, expected chores, and financial responsibilities, both parties need to discuss and agree upon behavioral expectations. This will include but not be limited to entertaining friends, curfews, and use of family vehicles. It has to be made clear that behaviors that were acceptable on campus, may not be permitted in your home.

Impact on Siblings

When an older child returns to live at home, it clearly changes the dynamics of the family. This change not only affects the parents and the returning young adult, it also significantly impacts the other, typically younger, siblings. The changed dynamics may result in the following:

- A younger sibling may resent the intrusion of the returning sibling, as she may have had "the rule of the roost" in the older sibling's absence. Now the bathroom and the TV and other resources have to be shared.

- In some cases, the younger sibling will not appreciate the returning sibling coaching the parents on how they are raising their children.

- The younger sibling may want the same rules of the house that apply to the returning young adult now applied to her. ("If Judy can stay out 'til 2 a.m. and have a beer, why can't I?")

- On the other hand, the younger sibling could appreciate the new, more mature, connection with the older sibling and might benefit from her mentorship (as it would not be surprising that the younger sibling is not listening too intently to her parents).

In order to successfully navigate this change in the home structure, the parents should call a family meeting to discuss the situation. This allows all parties to provide their input, communicate their feelings, and clearly discuss the behavioral expectations of the parents. It is better to discuss and negotiate the change in the family living situation when everyone is calm than to begin the discussion as a result of a conflict.

Impact on Family Finances

According to Tobias Financial Advisors, in an article by Kristen Grind that appeared in the May 3, 2013, edition of *The Wall Street Journal's* Money Beat, "Mother Can You Spare a Room?," hosting an adult-age child at home can cost $8,000 to $18,000 a year. Parents need to be firm with their returning adult children by having them pay toward the rent or mortgage. Other expenses, such as food and utilities, should be delineated in a budget. Some advisors suggest that parents draw up an actual contract and have the young adult sign it. Included in the contract are the requirements to procure a part-time job initially and ultimately a full-time job, as well as to cover some family bills.

Non-financial Contributions

If the young adult is having a problem finding a job, he should find a way to contribute to the household by doing the shopping, cleaning the house, picking up siblings from school, and even preparing meals. These non-financial activities contribute to the household culture and could defray some expenses. In cases where the parents cannot get the young adult to leave after eighteen months, Benjamin Tobias, president of Tobias Financial

Partners, suggests engaging in family therapy that is focused on encouraging the young adult to become more self-sufficient.

Developing an Exit Strategy

According to the existing literature, the biggest mistake parents make in this arena is failing to immediately establish a time frame for how long the young adult is allowed to stay. As mentioned in the *Wall Street Journal* article, the maximum time allowed should be eighteen months. Some advisors suggest no more than six months. Understand that the longer the young adult stays, the harder it will be to get her to leave. Early on you need to articulate your expectations to her. You expect her to get a job that can support her expenses and make payments toward her outstanding loans. It is possible that you may need the assistance of a behavioral specialist to develop an exit strategy for your returning young adult.

If the young adult is employed, the question is "How long before he can afford to live on his own?" As he moves up the corporate ladder or changes jobs, there needs to be an agreed-upon income level that would permit him to "exit" your home. One consideration may be to have a roommate or roommates to share the living expenses. Cary knows of a number of situations in which recent graduates have temporarily shared an apartment with friends or co-workers in order to afford the rent and cover their living expenses.

Timetable and Goals

It may seem cruel, but as a parent, you need to sit down with your child when he returns from college and develop a timeline that lasts no longer than eighteen months. The aim is motivating him to find a job and an affordable apartment, and to pay down college loans. The attainment of these goals should be realistic and based on the SMART goals discussed in Chapter One. Unless there is a timeline and accountability, goals will not be attained, and your recent graduate will become a permanent tenant in your home. The goals for your graduate should include:

- Determining a "move-out-by" date.
- Developing a resume and cover letter.
- Contacting their college or graduate school placement office to access job postings.
- Engaging in a job search by posting their resume on online job sites.
- Participating in local job fairs.
- Setting up interviews, networking with friends and business contacts each week.
- Obtaining a part-time job that produces discretionary income to cover personal expenses.
- Once employed, finding an affordable apartment and possibly one or more roommates.

Laying out and agreeing upon these specific, time-bound goals will aid your recent graduate in finding a job, exiting your home, and regaining his independence.

Lessons Learned

- There is a good chance that your son or daughter might have to move back home after college or graduate school in order to pay off educational loans or otherwise meet their financial needs.

- A discussion regarding the ground rules should take place prior to the graduate returning home.

- When the graduate returns to your home, you need to discuss financial responsibilities and the strategy for following the timeline for moving out. Many experts suggest that the maximum time an adult should be allowed to remain in your home after graduation is eighteen months.

- Understand that this return of the graduate will impact the "family chemistry" that currently exists. The other children who are still at home need to be involved in the discussions. Their concerns need to be heard.

- If the young adult is resistant to leave, it is time to engage the services of a family therapist to assist in developing an exit strategy.

Chapter Seven

Marriage Negotiations

After dating for a number of years, Jane and Randy decide to formalize their relationship and get married. They both have been married previously and each has adolescent children. Jane is Catholic and Randy is Jewish; they cannot agree on who will officiate at their wedding, the location of the ceremony, and what holidays they will celebrate together. It is apparent that these issues need to be resolved before they marry. One question before them is: who will assist them in resolving these issues, a religious leader or a marriage counselor?

The focus of this chapter is on the different stages of a relationship that build toward formalizing the union in marriage. At each of these stages, important negotiations need to take place between the partners and their parents, their religious leaders, their children (if they have them), and even their friends. Many partners may refer to these negotiations as arguments and conflicts. In actuality, these differences are opportunities to strengthen the relationship by reaching compromise through increased communication. These types of negotiations relate to many external and internal pressures that couples have to deal with and manage.

We also examine the initial nuptials, second marriages, interracial, interfaith, and same sex marriages. Negotiations that need to take place—before, during, and after marriage—are examined as well, including the purchase of a home.

Pre-marriage Negotiations

When couples are in the dating phase of their relationship and considering marriage, they need to communicate, especially when a conflict arises. If either party fails to clearly communicate during these situations, it could be a sign that there is a problem that should be addressed with a mental health professional.

Before partners decide to get married, their relationship needs to evolve and mature. When the partners choose to formalize their relationship, they must confront and negotiate a myriad of topics. These include but are not limited to: whether, when, and how many children they will have and how the children will be raised. Larry knows of a situation in which after the couple was married, the wife became pregnant and informed her husband that she was going to be a stay-at-home mom and no longer pursue her career. This announcement came as a complete surprise to her husband and caused conflict in their marriage. Obviously this topic had not been broached prior to their marriage as it should have been.

Other pre-marriage negotiations involve when to get married and whether to plan a traditional or "destination" wedding. Potential areas of conflict include: who gets invited, who pays for what, and where the couple will honeymoon and eventually live. The Millennial Generation, saddled with debt, has been opting for smaller, less expensive, destination weddings. Each option has hidden potential conflicts that should be fully discussed and negotiated. These negotiations are "layered," since more than two people are involved (such as parents, siblings, children, and even friends) who can influence the decisions.

A commonly asked question is, "Who should I negotiate with first?" The answer is: your prospective spouse. The couple must reach consensus on each of these issues. This is your wedding ceremony, and it should reflect your wishes and those of your partner. Be prepared for pushback from relatives and friends. Once you and your partner have made your decisions, you should remain steadfast and defend your position against the potential criticism of others. On the other hand, some of the input from others (relatives and friends) may include valid issues you may have not considered. This will result in additional negotiations with your partner. In order to present a united position when you respond to others' input at a later time, these conversations should include only you and your partner.

Relatives and friends may play the divide-and-conquer game by trying to influence one of you. Now is the time to stand together and only consider suggestions that would enhance your celebration, not those that detract from it. When the couple is paying for their own wedding, it is easier to deflect the many suggestions that will be made by parents, relatives, and friends. Even when the partners are not paying the bills, it is their wedding and it should primarily satisfy their needs and desires. The locus of your power is the fact that this is your wedding, not theirs.

Prior to negotiating with the sets of parents, you need to prepare by identifying those items that are negotiable and those that are not. In some instances, the parents will request that the wedding be held in their faith community's worship space. This is an especially difficult decision if one partner does not share the same faith community. To maintain neutrality, the wedding of Cary and his wife Susie was performed at a congregation that neither family belonged to. It happened that the rabbi who officiated at the ceremony was present when Susie and Cary met at a winter party, and having him officiate was a concession that satisfied both families.

One strategy is to be proactive: sit down with your parents and inform them of your wedding plans. If they wish to aid you financially, remember that financial assistance usually comes with "strings attached," including requests to influence your guest list, the venue, and your celebration.

Parents on both sides will want to add to your invitation list and/or influence the ceremony. If parents have divorced and remarried, it can even get more complicated.

When Larry gave a toast at his older son's marriage, his opening remark was: "Planning a wedding is not the best way to begin a marriage."

Today couples often wait until they have reached some point of economic success before getting married. This may, in part, explain why marriage remains more successful among upper socioeconomic groups. With these partners marrying later in life, the decision to have children may be delayed as their careers are developed and college loans are paid off. When the decision is made to have children, couples often may have advanced to a point in their careers where they can decide to telecommute, take an extended leave of absence, or even put their careers on hold. Recently many employers, such as Yahoo, have decided to offer extended maternity leave to both men and women. In many instances, mothers return to work after the child is in preschool. In other cases, the father decides to assume the role of Mr. Mom and stay home with the child. Cary is aware of a husband whose wife was a prominent gynecologist with a thriving practice, and the husband successfully raised their eight children. These are not typical relationships, but they illustrate a pattern that is growing among the Millennial Generation.

Prenuptial Agreements

Whether it is a first or second marriage, many couples enter into a prenuptial agreement. According to the FindLaw website, a prenup would be used to:

- Distinguish between separate and marital property.
- Protect the assets of each party and their estate plans.
- Prevent one party from assuming the debts of the other party.

- Define how property will be distributed upon death.
- Cleary define financial rights and responsibilities during the marriage.
- Prevent long and costly disputes in case of a divorce.

These types of documents are governed by state law. In the absence of a prenup, each state's laws will determine how property is handled during and after the marriage. The advantage of a prenuptial agreement is that you can craft one to meet your particular needs.

This type of negotiation can be fraught with emotions, which could complicate reaching a mutually acceptable agreement. In her 2008 article "5 Realities About Prenuptial Agreements—Why Having One May Be a Bad Choice For Your Marriage," attorney Laurie Israel wrote, "Negotiating a prenuptial agreement may irrevocably corrode your marriage and has the potential to make divorce more likely."

Some of the downsides of negotiating a prenup are:

- The partner is perceived as demonstrating a lack of faith in the other and a lack of commitment to the marriage when pushing for a prenuptial agreement.
- The partner also presumes a lack of fairness from the other in case of a divorce.
- These types of negotiation dynamics set a bad pattern for the marriage.
- A prenuptial negotiation agreement is perceived as not "romantic."
- The perception of the agreement is made worse because lawyers are involved.

Overall, Israel's thesis is that prenuptial agreements upset the balance in the relationship in unexpected ways and will often have unintended negative consequences.

Prenuptial agreements may be more important when there is a second marriage, assets have been accumulated by the parties, and/or there are children from a previous relationship. An article on prenuptial agreements in www.FindLaw.com, titled (no author listed) "What Can and Cannot be Included in Prenuptial Agreements" stated, "In order to ensure that your children from the prior relationship inherit some of your accumulated property, it should be addressed in the prenup."

Negotiation in Marriage

One of the most important skills a partner needs to learn in order to have a successful marriage is the ability to effectively communicate and negotiate. Inevitably not every issue will have been discussed and resolved prior to the marriage ceremony. There is no such thing as a relationship without issues; all relationship have them. A healthy partnership is one in which the issues are managed.

With the divorce rate hovering at around 50 percent in the previous decade, many couples clearly are unable to deal with critical issues that impact their relationship. These are situations in which the partners are so far apart that communication has broken down and negotiation is not feasible.

Our view is that a successful marital negotiation is akin to a successful business deal. For example:

Ironworks Inc. and Acme Steel have been doing business together for twenty-five years. Ironworks manufactures steel widgets and Acme sells raw steel. These two companies have worked together for all this time for two basic reasons:

1. They have a symbiotic relationship: they need each other.

2. The money is right. Ironworks believes they are buying their raw materials at a reasonable price and Acme believes they are selling their steel at an acceptable price.

Since these companies are privately held businesses, it is likely that they each desire to increase their profits. However, if Acme notifies Ironworks that next month the price per ton of steel will increase 50 percent, Ironworks may grudgingly place its next order but will immediately begin searching for a new supplier. By the same token, if Ironworks notifies Acme that next month they will pay 50 percent less per ton of steel, Acme may reluctantly fill the next order but will immediately begin searching for a new customer. Thus if either company substantially alters the price in its favor, a business relationship that had endured a quarter-century will collapse.

This hypothetical situation regarding these two companies closely relates to marriage. When the two companies conducted business with each other such that both were satisfied (not necessarily overjoyed) with the financial arrangement, the business relationship prospered. When either company attempted to seek a greater profit, a "win," the relationship was negatively impacted and potentially dissolved.

Similarly, when partners interact in a spirit of compromise and cooperation, their unions flourish. However, when one or both partners argue to "win," or frequently issues edicts or ultimatums, or threatens divorce if he doesn't get his way, the balance is upset and the marriage is threatened. Like the long-term business relationship between Ironworks Inc. and Acme Steel, marriage works best when each party strives for mutual satisfaction, not personal wins. Therefore, achieving "okay" in marriage is "great."

Discussions are necessary in any relationship to allow the relationship to grow, but the process must be constructive. Destructive arguing consists of raised voices, demeaning statements, and discounting the other party's viewpoint. Destructive arguing leads to resentment, a desire to get even, and ongoing issues that are never resolved. With constructive arguing, the goal is resolution or compromise, not finding a winner or a loser.

In his practice, Larry recommends five guidelines specific to marital communication and negotiation:

1. Partners should set aside an agreed-upon time to discuss an issue or area of disagreement. Most marital spats are spontaneous, when one party is upset and the other party is caught off guard. Resolution is rarely achieved in these types of "ambush" arguments. Delaying the discussion to a better time allows the partners to consider the issue more rationally and then negotiate in a more civil manner.

2. During the agreed-upon time, one and only one issue should be discussed at a time. When most partners argue, usually every other issue they have very quickly gets dumped into the conversation. Resolution is then impossible. These guidelines can help partners stay on track with a single issue:

    • No "side tracking" (getting off the issue)

    • No "bombs" (making an inflammatory comment)

    • No "digging up the museum" (bringing up an old, sore issue)

    Each partner must strive to speak only about the specific issue at hand until it is resolved.

3. It is easier to settle issues when partners learn to speak concretely, in specifics rather than in general terms. The questions that need to be considered are: "What does it look like? What would I see?" For example, if the wife tells the husband she would like him to be "more affectionate," the husband should not respond, "You don't know what you are talking about; I'm as affectionate as the next guy." The husband could instead say, "Dear, if I were more affectionate, what would it look like? What would we see?" The wife, then, could answer with whatever behaviors she would see as affectionate, such as holding hands, writing her a love note, bringing flowers, rubbing her back, fixing the sink, arranging a date (including securing the babysitter), etc.

4. Always use active listening. For many couples, arguing entails over-shouting, interrupting, threatening, and using negative body

language. If one party is silent, often he or she is not listening to what the other partner is saying but is focused on responding as soon as there is an opening. Active listening is clearly not taking place.

5. Use the paraphrase technique, which involves having one partner state his position for no more than sixty seconds while the other partner quietly listens. At the end of the minute, before the second partner can offer a rebuttal, she must paraphrase the other partner's position. This forces the partner to really "hear." Once the paraphrase is stated, the first partner must affirm that the paraphrase is accurate and then the second partner gets sixty seconds to state her position. The first partner then must, in turn, listen and paraphrase. This process facilitates "active listening."

By using these five recommended guidelines for communication and negotiation, couples can resolve their conflicts in a constructive manner, which will allow their relationship to grow and flourish.

Second Marriages

Earlier in this chapter, we noted the challenges of second marriages with respect to a prenuptial agreement. A number of other topics also need to be negotiated when entering into a second marriage. This is especially true if both spouses have their own homes and/or are bringing children into the marriage.

Counseling is strongly advised for couples when the marriage will be a second one for one or both partners. You might think you are older, wiser, more mature, know better what you want or don't want, and have learned from your mistakes. Common sense suggests that second marriages would succeed at a higher rate than first ones. Nevertheless, current demographic data indicates that second marriages fail 65 percent of the time, in contrast to the 50 percent failure rate for first unions. Among the basic reasons second marriages struggle to succeed: financial stress, ex-in-laws, stepchildren, biological children, and hostile ex-spouses hoping to sabotage the new relationship.

Subsequent marriages falter for another major reason. Partners bring some of the same characteristics that probably played a role in the demise of the first relationship into the new one. The psychoanalytic school of thought argues that the person we pair with is essentially predestined. We unconsciously seek people with certain personality features. Thus in a second marriage, we must become mindful of our role in the breakup of the first marriage and also become aware of the traits in our spouse that contributed to that breakup. Without counseling, most divorced people remain ignorant of their issues, blame their ex-spouse for the dissolution of the first marriage, find a new partner with many of the characteristics of their ex-spouse, and recreate another strained relationship.

Partners need to determine where they will live as a family—an existing home of one of the spouses or a new residence. In Cary's case, he sold his home and moved into his new wife's home. In order to accommodate his son, who had just gone away to college, a portion of the basement was finished into an office/guest room. A number of pieces of Cary's furniture and paintings were moved into the new room, but most of his prior home's furnishings were sold or donated to a local charity.

When two homes are combined, the negotiations begin. Topics to be discussed include: what goes or stays, and where things should be placed. The challenge is that one person has moved into another person's home and is now a new member of someone's household. The strategy Cary used successfully was to first adjust to the change of address and then begin to make changes that both parties agreed would make it their home. In Cary's case, besides the addition of an office/guest room, the den was refurbished, the sunroom was expanded, and a new patio was installed. The decorating was updated and a number of pieces of furniture were replaced. Over time, these changes transformed his wife's home into *their* home.

Some Additional Challenges

Past experiences and behaviors. In addition to the living space, a more daunting set of challenges is changing attitudes and extinguishing past experiences with a previous spouse. As stated earlier, both parties bring to the new relationship their positive and negative experiences from their previous marriages. In many cases, a certain word or even an action will engender a negative response. Each partner has experienced situations in his or her previous relationships, including the prior marriage, that have left "scars." In many cases, the person has yet to completely heal. In a previous chapter, we discussed "hot buttons" and how they can cause a conflict to arise. Unless you know your new partner's hot buttons, there is no doubt that you will inadvertently push them from time to time.

One approach to preventing these hot buttons from causing conflict and damaging the relationship is to seek out counseling as mentioned earlier. Premarital counseling is a good investment. The counselor can serve as a mediator and assist the parties in identifying and resolving their issues. In Cary's case, his future wife stated, "If we are going to marry, then we must have premarital counseling." In his case it was non-negotiable; counseling was a must, since both divorces had been fraught with conflict and anger.

Using a professional counselor permits you to offload the negative "baggage" that you would have introduced into the new marriage. As mentioned earlier, second marriages often fail because the behaviors that destroyed the first marriage have not been dealt with and/or extinguished. If they did not work the first time, why would they work this time? This is a question that needs to be addressed prior to entering into a new marriage and relationship. You need to realize that you are dealing with a different person, a different personality, and what didn't work the first time needs to be replaced with different behaviors. Neither party to this second marriage wants to pay the emotional debts incurred by the previous spouse. By participating in premarital counseling, a couple can reduce the risk of repeating the mistakes made in the previous marriage or relationship. They will also learn techniques to enhance their communication skills.

The children. All too often, second marriages can be negatively impacted by the attitudes and loyalties of young and even the adult children from the previous marriage. In many cases, these children are conflicted. They want their parents to be happy, but they are not always accepting of the new spouse. Some younger children blame themselves for the divorce and engage in "magical thinking," believing that if they act in a certain manner, they can prevent or reverse the second marriage and get their parents back together again. This behavior has to be confronted by the parent or, if necessary, approached with the assistance of a family psychologist or other licensed counselor. An unhappy child can have a negative impact on or even destroy the second marriage.

Adolescent and adult children can be a major challenge in a blended family. They have built up loyalties, will tend to align themselves with their parent, and may not accept the new stepparent. We know of more than one case where the adolescent or adult child did not accept the new spouse and became disruptive or tried to negatively impact the relationship. This behavior puts the new spouse in a tenuous position. While building a relationship with a new partner, the spouse must gain the trust and respect of the partner's children. In many cases, the children are themselves conflicted and believe that by accepting their father's or mother's new partner, they are rejecting their other biological parent. This is an opportunity for family counseling to air out the issues and find areas of agreement.

The child has to come to the realization that the marriage is going to happen. If she desires a positive relationship with the biological parent, she needs to accept that parent's new partner. On the other hand, the new partner has to accept the fact that he is not the child's biological parent and must earn the child's trust and respect.

Cary had to earn his stepdaughter's respect and love. After seeing her mother happy in the new relationship and having the opportunity to interact with Cary on a regular basis for an extended period of time, the stepdaughter allowed the relationship to mature and grow. Cary would never be her father, but he became her "Pops" and an integral part of her life.

When a child refuses to accept the new partner, the biological parent needs to inform the child that the marriage will happen. It is a "gravity issue"—a situation that will not change, and the child's behavior will not impact anything, except the relationship between the biological parent and the child. The child and the new partner need to find a "common ground" on which they can build a relationship.

In one case the authors are familiar with, the adult daughter of the husband would not accept the new partner. This greatly troubled the father and the potential spouse and caused some conflict. The daughter's goal was probably to disrupt and possibly destroy the relationship. Her anger from the breakup of her parents' marriage was the basis of her objections to the new partner. Again, the stance the father needed to take was that his daughter should be as concerned with his happiness as she was for her own.

Discipline. In second marriages and blended families, all too often parents adopt a system where only the biological parent can discipline a biological child. This structure is doomed to failure because it is unwieldy and doesn't work. What do you do if the stepchild is misbehaving and the biological parent is not present? Moreover, this arrangement continues to emphasize the fact that this "family" is truly split. Parents of a blended family must clearly communicate that the "family" is a unit and as such any child can go to any parent and any parent can redirect any child. Before you decide to marry someone, you must be assured that your new partner agrees to this philosophy.

Interfaith Marriages

The number of interfaith marriages has increased among the members of the Millennial Generation. According to an article written by Jessica Grose, "Married Interfaith Couples Who Keep Religious Traditions Separate on the Rise," which appeared in the February 4, 2014, issue of *What Women Really Think*, a quarter of Millennials were religiously unaffiliated when they were young adults, compared to 13 percent of boomers. The same article reported that David McClendon, a PhD student at the University of Texas at Austin, found that 40 percent of couples married in the current decade are keeping their own religious traditions, as compared to just over 20 percent in the 1960s. An article published in April 2013 in *The New York Times* titled "Interfaith Unions: A Mixed Blessing, "by Naomi Schaefer Riley, stated, "The older you are when you wed, the more likely you will marry outside your faith." The statistic Cary found most interesting was that over 67 percent of individuals between the ages of 36 and 45 entered into an interfaith union.

This creates additional issues to be negotiated, including but not limited to:

- Who will officiate at the wedding?
- What religion will the couple practice?
- In what faith will the children be raised?

Who will officiate? In an interfaith marriage, the biggest negotiation that takes place is between the engaged couple and their parents regarding their desire to marry outside their faith community. Parents can be "myopic" and insist that their children not marry outside their faith. Cary has heard parents state that they would not attend the ceremony unless it was in a church, synagogue, or mosque, as the case may be. In many situations, clergy will not perform a mixed-marriage wedding. Sometimes a compromise is a wedding performed by a judge and attended by a priest, minister, or rabbi who offers ceremonial blessings while not performing the actual marriage ceremony. In some instances, a friend of the couple obtains the necessary authorization over the Internet to permit him or her to officiate at the wedding.

In the Jewish faith, a number of Reform and Reconstructionist rabbis, including some who are not affiliated with congregations, will officiate over a mixed marriage as long as the husband and wife agree to raise the children in a Jewish home. This same condition holds true in the Roman Catholic Church. Cary has attended a number of weddings where a rabbi was found on the Internet and performed the ceremony at a location other than a synagogue. In more than one instance, clergy from other faith communities were present, but only offered a prayer and did not marry the couple.

Prior to getting married, there must be a discussion as to who will officiate and where the marriage will take place. There will most likely be a need to compromise along the way. In Cary's first marriage, the bride was from an Orthodox Jewish background. His family was more liberal in their practice, did not keep a kosher home, and worked on the Sabbath. Her family was much more observant and maintained a kosher home. When they decided where to hold the wedding, it was important to find a synagogue that was acceptable to both families. Cary's parents insisted that men and women sit together, but her family wanted a ceremony where the men and women sat in different areas. To better explain this situation, we must take a phrase from the musical *Fiddler on the Roof*, "Tradition, tradition that is what it's about." The two families reached a compromise: rabbis from the bride's family participated in the marriage ceremony and a separate area was provided, separated by a curtain, for the Orthodox members of her family.

What religion will you practice? Will one partner be encouraged to convert, or will they both maintain their religious affiliations? In her article "Interfaith Unions: A Mixed Blessing," Naomi Schaefer Riley said that fewer than 50 percent of the interfaith couples surveyed discussed what faith they would practice prior to their marriage. She also found that over 80 percent of the survey participants felt having the same values was more important than having the same religion.

First, the individuals planning to marry need to discuss their religious differences with each other. Once they agree on a path, they need to negotiate with their parents. When the parents of the partners actively practice different religions, the negotiation becomes more complex and the number of individuals involved is usually larger. To use a negotiation term, there are a "significant number of constituents involved." Finally, they will have to meet with their clergy and learn what hurdles they need to clear if one of the partners decides to convert to their partner's religion. Frequently this will require the partner who wishes to convert to complete a series of classes on the new religion, and the couple to receive counseling from the clergy prior to the wedding ceremony. Most clergy are trained to help partners through these difficult and sometimes stressful negotiations.

Once the couple decides if they are going to practice one religion or both, they can determine how they will celebrate the various religious holidays. In the case of Cary's son's marriage, they celebrate both Jewish and Christian holidays. They reached a compromise that satisfied both.

This negotiation topic can be very volatile and should be approached in a careful, respectful, and thoughtful manner. Even if the partner practices the same religion, for example Judaism, there are a number of levels of observance that could be a source of conflict.

What religion will the children practice? After partners in an interfaith marriage have reached an understanding about what religion they will each practice and which religious traditions they will observe in their home, they need to reach an agreement about what religion their children will practice. Couples need to seriously address this topic prior to the union.

If a Jewish man marries a Roman Catholic woman, for example, will they raise their children Catholic or Jewish? According to traditional Jewish practice, the religion of the mother determines the child's religion. If the child is baptized, however, then he is welcomed into the Catholic religious family. In some cases, the philosophy of the parents is to expose their children to both religions and let them choose their own path as they get older.

Cary knows of a situation when the child of a mixed marriage began religious school, the parent who practiced the other faith felt threatened. The marriage began to experience stress and conflict, which caused a breakdown in communication between the partners. A feeling of betrayal developed, and, ultimately, the couple divorced.

In many cases, not only is the couple involved in what religion the children should practice, but the grandparents, and sometimes their siblings, often also weigh in on the discussion. This puts pressure on the partners; it can cause conflict and raise questions about family tradition and loyalties. The more people involved, the more complex the negotiation. This agreement should be one that suits the couple's needs, not those of other parties.

One strategy is to use a three-column planning sheet. The first column indicates the subjects that you agree on, the second column shows where there is disagreement, and the third column indicates where each partner has compromised. In this manner, all the issues are identified and "on the table" to be discussed openly. This can be done between the partners or with an intermediary or a coach. In many instances, a marriage counselor, psychologist, or clergyperson can assist the couple through this process. This approach would isolate the religious issues regarding the raising of the children. It would permit each partner to offer one or more potential solutions and increase the level of communication.

This situation is even more of a challenge if this is a second marriage and one spouse already has children of a different faith from the prior marriage. The question that needs to be addressed is: will there be children of different religions under the same roof? If so, that could cause confusion and potential conflict. This question needs to be addressed prior to the union, and a decision must be made before any additional children are born. There is no doubt that pressure will be brought by both sets of future grandparents as to the child's religion. The decision is to be made by the parents, not by the grandparents. In some cases, these "mixed" marriages take place after the children from the previous marriage are grown, married, and out of the home. The rule here should be what is in the best interest of the children, siblings, and parents, not the larger family. Remember, collaboration and compromise are signs of strength, not weakness, and any decision needs to reflect both parties' input.

Interracial Marriages

When a marriage includes individuals of different racial backgrounds, there are challenges to both the partners and their families. They say love is "colorblind." If the potential spouses are also of different religions, the situation is even more complicated. According to U.S. Census Bureau statistics, as reported in the article "Interracial Marriage in the US: Facts and Figures" in *The New Observer,* there were 275,500 interracial marriages in 2010. A June 2014 *Madame Noire* newsletter, written by Kimberly Gedeon, reported that interracial marriages have a 41 percent chance of ending in divorce versus a 31 percent for same-race marriages.

Some of the issues that interracial partners face are detailed in "10 Pitfalls About Interracial Relationships" by Rishona Campbell on www.rishona.net in December 2011. We will discuss each issue and provide strategies to deal with it.

1. *Yourself.* When entering into an interracial relationship, ask yourself some questions.

    a. Do you have the strength, courage, and tenacity to deal with the issues posed by an interracial relationship?

    b. Will you be able to deal with criticism from your family, friends, and co-workers?

    c. How will you deal with public disdain?

2. *Family.* Many people could care less what others think, while some are very impacted by the opinions of others, especially if they are family members.

    a. Maintain the position that you should be respected by all parties.

    b. Remember you are in a relationship with a person, not their family.

    c. Your significant other should support you when his or her family is overly critical.

3. *The public.* You have no control or influence over how strangers treat you.

   a. Elect to ignore such people.

   b. Don't in any way let them diminish your status.

4. *The community of people of color.* Unfortunately, this community will often label those who date outside their race as "sellouts."

   a. Once again, elect to ignore such people.

   b. You are not required to defend your decision to marry outside your race.

5. *Other interracial partners.* Remember that others who date interracially are not automatically your allies.

   a. Be wary of those who make judgments about your relationship.

   b. Interracial or not, no two romantic relationships are the same.

   c. Look out for people who imply interracial relationships are "ideal," "preferred," or "superior."

6. *Stereotypes.* You cannot discount the power of stereotypes if you are in an interracial relationship.

   a. Don't place a great deal of weight on these stereotypes. Be yourself.

   b. Do not buy in to disparaging stereotypical comments about you or your relationship.

   c. As interracial partners, you also have to examine the stereotypes that you may hold about each other.

7. *Fetish vs. Attraction.* Basic questions that each partner to this union needs to ask include:

   a. How does the other person see me?

   b. When will I meet my partner's family and close friends?

   c. Am I seen as a potential partner or as their next adventure?

8. *Educating.* You and your partner should prepare yourselves for a steep learning curve.

   a. You and your partner need to know when not to take things personally.

b. Be ready to address questions from friends about customs, your heritage, and your body.

c. Your peers need to know you are not a trailblazer.

9. *Making a statement.* You are blessed whenever someone loves you.

a. You have no control over what other people think of you.

b. Stay focused on your relationship.

c. Only you and your partner know the true nature of your relationship.

10. *Know your ultimate desires.* Be realistic.

a. Identify the issues you are willing to compromise on and deal with.

b. Communicate with your partner to verify that you both want the same things from the relationship.

Same Sex Marriages

Many of the challenges discussed previously in this chapter are faced by same sex partners when they enter into a marriage or civil union. In addition to negotiating with each other and their parents, if they desire a religious wedding, they need to find a member of the clergy that will marry them. Since the United States Supreme Court has legalized same sex marriages, they now must be recognized by every state.

Many clergy will officiate at same sex marriages if both members of the union are of the same religion. There are other faith communities that do not countenance same sex marriages and will still not recognize the union. However, some members of the clergy may be willing to bless the marriage.

According to experts in the field of psychology, same sex partners experience the same relationship problems in marriages as do heterosexual partners, including having to work out how their natural or adopted children will be raised. Now that same sex marriage is legal, when same sex partners decide to divorce, they are subject to the same marital laws, including the disposition of assets, as are other couples. Therefore, many of the same emotional and financial topics will need to confronted and negotiated if the union is terminated.

Buying a House

Today, many couples purchase a house prior to getting married. We define "house" as a condo, co-op, or single-family home. The process will involve several negotiations between the parties purchasing the home. The first negotiation should be agreeing upon the parameters of the property they are hoping to buy. The second negotiation, a multi-tiered one, would be among the buyers and the seller (or the seller's agent), and the lending organization.

In the first negotiation, the couple will need to determine the following:

- Location (city or suburban)
- Price range and source of financing
- Monthly expenses (rent or mortgage, utilities, etc.)
- Number of bedrooms, bathrooms, etc.
- Type (ranch, multi-story, multi-family, townhouse, new construction)
- Design (modern, traditional, colonial)

Once these issues have been put on the table and discussed, the couple needs to reach some level of agreement on each issue. The next step after the partners agree on the above checklist is to meet with a lending organization and determine how much they can borrow. This outcome will impact their ability to purchase the home they desire. If they are approved by a lending organization, they can bring the preapproval letter with them when they meet with the realtor. At that point, they know what price range they can afford. They will have a clearer idea of how much their monthly payment will be and whether the offer they submit will be taken seriously.

An experienced realtor may, in some cases, function as a mediator between the partners if the issues of price, community, home type, and size had not been adequately addressed prior to their first meeting. In order to narrow the search and make the process more efficient, we recommend that partners work these issues out ahead of time. The Internet can assist the couple in being better prepared for their first meeting with a realtor.

Let your realtor assemble a list of homes that meet the criteria that you and your partner have decided upon. The realtor can then begin to set up appointments for showings, prioritizing the showings by starting with the homes that you may *not* desire and moving to the homes you really think you want. The reason for this prioritization is to allow you to gain experience dealing with the homeowner (if it is a "for sale by owner" situation), or with an agent representing the owner, while gathering information that will be critical to your final negotiation and decision.

After you have completed your search, you will want to develop your initial offer based, in part, on the amount of funds preapproved by your financial organization. Included in this offer would be deductions from the initial offering for the following:

- Items that need to be repaired or replaced (heating/cooling units, appliances, dated fixtures in bathrooms and kitchens, etc.)
- Comparable listings for homes that sold in that area

Documenting these deductions in your offer will explain and defend how you arrived at your initial offer.

After the initial offer, and perhaps the receipt of a counter offer from the seller's realtor, you may have reached an agreed-upon purchase price. After the inspection is completed and the report published, you may elect to counter based upon the cost to bring the home up to current codes and standards. In many states, inspection by an independent inspector prior to the sale is mandatory. This protects the buyer from unethical sellers and reduces the potential for litigation after the sale is completed.

Lessons Learned

- Sometimes the greatest negotiation challenges occur before you get married. Planning a wedding and interacting with parents and friends provide opportunities to negotiate compromises and produce a win-win result. The future spouses first must reach agreement on all the major issues; then they can present a united front to others who may wish to influence their decisions. These negotiations provide an opportunity to increase communication between the partners.

- Open and honest communication is a critical aspect of a healthy marriage. Too many couples believe that their problems will improve or disappear after they are married. A wedding does not resolve issues; in fact, in most cases, unresolved problems get worse and can eventually lead to conflict and divorce.

- When partners interact in a spirit of respect, compromise, and cooperation, the union flourishes. However, when either partner argues to "win," frequently issues edicts or ultimatums, or threatens divorce, the balance is upset and the marriage is threatened. Marriage works best when each party strives for mutual satisfaction rather than a personal win.

- Prenuptial agreements are governed by state law. In the absence of a prenup, state laws determine how property is handled during and after the marriage. The advantage of prenuptial agreements is that you can craft them to meet your specific needs.

- Prenuptial agreements may be more necessary prior to a second marriage, especially when there are children from a previous relationship. They are designed to ensure that children from a first union inherit some of their parent's property, which should be detailed in the prenup.

- Destructive arguing consists of raised voices, demeaning words, and a discounting attitude. This type of a communication pattern leads to resentment, a desire to get even, and ongoing issues that never end. With constructive arguing, the goal is resolution or compromise, not finding a winner or a loser.

- Parents must realize that when they enter into a second marriage, their children are part of the new relationship. Parents have to prepare their children for the challenges of the new union.

(continued)

- Prior to entering into a new union, the potential partners should seriously consider premarital counseling to rid them of the "baggage" from the previous relationship and to build on the strengths of the new relationship.

- New stepparents must recognize that building trust and a relationship with their partner's adolescent or adult children prior to and during their new marriage is critical.

- Interfaith marriages have grown among the Millennial Generation. When members of this generation decide to formalize their relationship through marriage, there are many issues to be discussed and ultimately negotiated. These issues include: who will officiate at the wedding, what religion(s) will be practiced in the home, and in what faith potential children will be raised.

- Potential spouses entering an interracial or same sex marriage will face many of the same challenges as those entering an interfaith marriage, as well as some additional challenges.

- Buying a new house is a challenge for both married couples and for couples sharing a home. In fact, buying a home is a complicated negotiation involving multiple issues, such as location, price, and the size of the home. These and other issues need to be resolved between the parties and the realtor prior to selecting a home.

Chapter Eight

Negotiating a Divorce

Sam and Helen have been married for over twenty years and have enjoyed the benefits of Sam's career as a captain at a major international airline. On average, Sam was gone up to half the month flying between their home and destinations in Europe. Now that Sam is retired and spends a great deal of time at home, Helen finds that she is no longer free to do as she pleases. This change in lifestyle has led to recurring conflicts and a reduction in intimacy. They were not able to adjust to the change in lifestyle and ultimately divorced.

Based on the current high rate of divorce, most divorced couples apparently did not have the opportunity or the ability to effectively communicate, resolve conflicts, or negotiate. If there are no children involved with the divorce, the parties could essentially go their separate ways after the dissolution of the marriage and have little or no contact with each other. However, divorced couples who had children together, or are in business together, will have to interact together for years to come. There will be medical decisions, school plays, concerts, teacher conferences, sporting events, recitals, graduations, and, hopefully, weddings and childbirths. If they are business partners, there will be many business decisions they will have to make together. Given all these future events, these partners will still need to learn to communicate and negotiate civilly despite being divorced. If not, many of these events, which should be happy times, could become disasters and have a negative impact on their children's emotional and social development as well as their academic performance.

Resolving Conflicts

As we interviewed a number of individuals who have been or are going through a divorce, one thing became apparent: these individuals and their ex-spouses had difficulties resolving conflicts. One divorcee stated, "Before we got married, I had no idea that when a conflict arose, my husband would not communicate with me—he would just shut down." They had not experienced a serious conflict during the courtship, so she no idea about how he would respond to a disagreement. She told Larry that if she had known her husband would withdraw in such a manner, she would not have married him. It is unfortunate that during the courtship she did not ask him how his parents handled disputes and conflict. This may have provided a window into the future of their relationship.

Research on divorce indicates that most partners (approximately 80 percent) settle into a groove within eighteen months to two years after the final divorce decree. For the sake of the children, they learn to communicate civilly and negotiate reasonably with each other.

Dealing with Anger

Unfortunately, the data also suggests that 15 to 20 percent of divorced couples with children continue to fight and argue, sometimes for years after the final divorce decree. Sadly, Larry has observed in his practice that many of these acrimonious partners continue to communicate and negotiate in the same maladaptive manner that played a large part in the demise of the original relationship. To make matters worse, these angry partners often bring the children into their conflict.

Most adults would agree that effective parents are those who put their personal needs secondary to the needs of their child. With some divorced parents, though, it is almost as if their anger and frustration supersedes the best interest of their child. These parents express their anger and frustration frequently and openly, which can be harmful to the child. Unfortunately, some divorced parents act as if they hate their ex-spouse more than they love their children.

Effective communication and negotiation between divorced partners is especially difficult because of hurt feelings. Someone you once loved and even had a child with now rejects you. Nevertheless, divorced parents must put aside their anger and distrust and strive to negotiate in good faith with their ex. They must do so not because they want to, but because they have to. If they let their frustration rule, they will likely be miserable for years, even decades, and their children will come to resent them as well.

It is not unusual that the child elects to identify with the non-aggressive parent and in some cases rejects the other parent in order to eliminate the conflict, drama, and chaos. In a case like this, the non-aggressive parent often assumes the role of a mediator and tries to assist the other parent in repairing the relationship with the child. Unless the negative behavior is extinguished, the child may not re-establish a relationship with the other parent. In a number of cases, a father or mother was not invited to the daughter's wedding due to the level of conflict between the parents. In one particular case, the father was told that if he tried to attend, he would be stopped by security. The earlier the anger is extinguished, the better the children will be able to maintain positive relationships with both parents.

Relationships are reciprocal, whether married or divorced. What you put out comes back. Divorced partners must understand this.

Negotiations between divorced partners should not be a competition or an opportunity for one-upmanship. A negotiation should be simple, straightforward, seeking compromise, and guided by the best interests of the child or children. By negotiating in this manner, the entire family unit will benefit.

Divorce Mediation

In some states, the courts mandate mediation for partners seeking a divorce. Many states also use a "no-fault divorce" or "collaborative divorce" concept in which no blame is placed on either party for the failure of the marriage. The purpose of the mediation process is to have the parties work out the settlement with the assistance of a neutral party. The mediator's job is to keep lines of communication open, help the parties brainstorm ideas, reality-test potential solutions, and assist the partners in their decision-making process. In some cases, there are lawyers involved, but the relationship is not adversarial and the parties are empowered to develop their own unique solutions to the questions of custody, visitation, financial support, and division of property. The mediation process is both flexible and confidential.

According to www.mediate.com, mediation brings about a higher level of communication between the parties, which can facilitate dealing with the critical issues pertaining to the children. This process has the ability to assist the parties in communication, which will ultimately benefit everyone after the divorce.

Collaborative Divorce

In a collaborative divorce, which is a voluntary process and can be more time-consuming than a traditional divorce, the parties are supported by a team of professionals, which could include a financial expert, a behavioral specialist (psychologist or social worker), and a specially trained attorney. These specialists provide information and guidance, permitting the parties to reach a mutually beneficial solution. The lynchpin to this process is the commitment to settlement by the lawyers and the parties.

There are four building blocks that support this process outlined by the Collaborative Family Law Council of Wisconsin on their web page, www.collabdivorce.com:

- A written pledge not to litigate in court
- Withdrawal if either party chooses to litigate
- Open and complete exchange of information
- Negotiation according to the priorities of all family members

These processes are designed to reduce the acrimony that results from an adversarial system and to stabilize the relationship. When discussing collaborative divorce, the term "interest-based negotiation" is often used; this approach focuses the parties on their underlying needs, wants, values, and objectives. Collaborative divorce is built around a process in which the parties negotiate the problem by exchanging information frankly and making the necessary concessions to reach an agreement. In this manner, the parties are in control of the process and the final crafting of the settlement.

In an earlier chapter, we referred to the importance of controlling one's emotions in a negotiation. Negotiations fail when an individual loses his composure and then his focus. If the negotiation/discussion gets heated, we suggest the strategy of making a statement such as "Unless we can treat each other with respect, I cannot see any reason to continue this discussion." Another statement could be "Let's select another time to talk; it appears that we need some time to regain our composure so we can have a constructive discussion."

As explained in an earlier discussion, there is a need for structure in these types of negotiations. A formal agenda is not necessary as this is not a business transaction, but some structure is needed.

If the negotiation/discussion is conducted in person, the parties should select a neutral setting where no one has a perceived power base. Both parties are free to leave at any time and not feel trapped in a person's home, office, or apartment. In addition, having such a discussion in a public place puts a premium on being respectful.

Occasionally the negotiation/discussion is conducted on the telephone. That can make it more difficult, as you cannot read the other person's body language, and you must then rely on the tone of the voice, the selection of language, and the tempo of the discussion to guide you.

The collaborative approach to divorce is usually less expensive for the parties, as there is no need to litigate and the process is more efficient. The parties negotiate each segment of the settlement, and if they reach an impasse, it is resolved with the guidance of the mediator. If this process fails, there is a mandatory mutual withdrawal of the attorneys, and new litigation counsel is hired.

Sometimes negotiations directly with the soon-to-be or the existing ex-spouse are difficult or impossible due to anger-based behavioral issues. In these instances, an attorney needs to be involved, and sometimes the courts also need to become involved. The withholding of alimony or child support to influence the outcome of any negotiation would violate an existing divorce agreement and would be illegal. Unfortunately, there are many cases in which the only way the parties could reach agreement was when the courts issued an order regarding support or alimony.

In a recent case shared with us, one partner in a same sex marriage took her child out of the jurisdiction without the other partner's consent, violating their state law. The other partner had to get the court to issue an order instructing the mother to return to the jurisdiction with the child. There was no opportunity for a negotiation, so the partner had no choice but to engage the assistance of the court. Her partner had no choice but to return to the jurisdiction with their daughter. These types of scenarios do not contribute to a positive relationship between the parties and do negatively impact the child.

When Children Are Involved

It is not uncommon for either party to a divorce to engage in power plays and coercive negotiating techniques. When children are involved in a divorce, they can become pawns in the negotiation and may be used to leverage an agreement from the other party. Any disagreement between the custodial parents should be settled with the assistance of their attorneys or a neutral party and not involve the children. This has to be one of the ground rules and should be articulated prior to any negotiation.

In some cases, one or both of the parties may use increased time with the children as a bargaining chip to gain other benefits. This subject should be seen as non-negotiable. Generally, both parties have the right of "equality" to see and spend time with their children. If such a chip is played, you may need to involve your attorney and possibly the courts to resolve the conflict. While this action will likely exacerbate the tension between the parties, it might be necessary.

Another subject often negotiated with the divorced partner is having the children on holidays. Sometimes there may be a need to trade or compromise on dates. Again, this may provide an opportunity for one ex-spouse to try to leverage the relationship and shift power. When a compromise or trade is made, the parties should determine whether it will be a "one time" event or how these decisions will be handled in the future

School conferences, therapy sessions, and medical appointments are other areas of potential conflict. These situations should be addressed in the divorce agreement, whether it is court-determined or a result of a negotiated agreement. Many school conferences and doctors' appointments are scheduled during the workday and may be inconvenient for both parents. Both parties should be given advance notice of appointments and conferences so they can adjust their calendars.

It is critical to the welfare of the children that pick-up and drop-off times be as consistent as possible. It is suggested, especially with younger children, that the exchange of children between parents be made at daycare or at school rather than the exchange taking place from one parent's home to the other parent's home.

Consistency and stability are important in these situations and are a basis of conflict if not adhered to. When participating in a collaborative divorce scenario, the parties will have negotiated ground rules pertaining to scheduling, child support, vacations, and alimony. Once there is an agreement, it must be maintained by both parties to the divorce. If in the future conditions change, the parties may renegotiate these ground rules.

Sometimes if a party does not get the financial support or the desired custody conditions in the settlement (or in court), one or both parties may be tempted to retaliate against the other in post-divorce negotiations.

Lessons Learned

- Communicating and negotiating effectively between divorced parties is especially difficult because of a history of hurt feelings. Divorced couples must put aside their anger and distrust and strive to negotiate in good faith. They must do so not because they want to, but because they have to. If frustration rules, they will likely be miserable for years, even decades, and as a result, their children may come to resent them.

- If possible, couples getting a divorce should consider a no-fault or collaborative divorce rather than the traditional divorce, which involves litigation. These alternatives could produce a more collaborative, less combative proceeding, resulting in an agreement that is best for the children and the parties. It also provides the parties an opportunity for improved communication and decision-making not solely influenced by emotion.

- Parties to a divorce should not engage in power plays and coercive negotiating techniques, especially when children are involved. Children should not become pawns in the negotiation and be used to leverage an agreement. Any disagreement is between the custodial parents and should not involve the children. This has to be one of the many ground rules that should be part of any divorce negotiation.

Chapter Nine

Negotiating with Aging Parents

Norman is ninety, lives in Florida, has Alzheimer's, and has just had another accident with his car. When his family finds out, they take away his keys and sell the car. After they return to their home, they find out that their dad took a cab to the local Cadillac dealership the next day and purchased a new car. They decide it is time Dad gives up his license, returns the car, and stops driving before he hurts someone, including himself. Since Norman is stubborn and sees driving as an important part of being independent, they know this will not be an easy discussion. This family conflict could have been prevented by having this discussion when Norman was more aware and competent.

As our parents age, they become more dependent on others for their care and safety. The adult children then take on the role of caregiver, guardian, and parents' advocate. This role reversal can be caused by medical issues, dementia, mental illness, and/or depression. This chapter will look at strategies that will permit you, as your parents' advocate, to ensure that your parents are protected, receive the needed medical assistance, and have their final wishes respected.

These types of negotiations are complicated by the fact that there is a power transfer between the generations and also potential role reversals. The parents will still feel they have legitimate power in their role as the parents and should be able to make their own decisions. Their adult children will have information power and access to the expert power provided by social workers, assisted living and senior living administrators, and physicians. Prior to any of the sensitive negotiations recommended in this chapter, the adult children should engage the assistance of these experts. These can be very sensitive discussions/negotiations, and detailed planning is a critical requirement, along with building a coalition among siblings and other key influencers prior to making any final decisions.

Negotiations can be made easier or even eliminated if there are appropriate discussions at earlier times. Strategies for such discussions will be suggested for each topic.

Giving Up the Car Keys

The ability to drive and own a car is a form of independence that is coveted by older adults. This is a very sensitive topic and needs to be raised by the adult children prior to the time they feel that their parent or parents no longer can drive safely. There are a number of clues that a parent's driving skill is diminishing, and they should not be ignored by the spouse or adult children.

You can't wait for an accident or major traffic violation to take action. You need to consider the danger to the parent or to other involved parties as well. The financial impact on the estate due to an accident, injuries, and/or death caused by a parent's poor driving also must be considered. The media have covered many incidents in which senior citizens have hit the gas pedal instead of the brake and driven through the front window of a store or restaurant, causing injuries and even death. Sadly, it is up to the adult children of senior citizens to prevent such tragedies.

According to the HelpGuide.org article "Age and Driving Safety Tips and Warning Signs for Older Drivers," the following questions need to be answered before you consider taking the car keys away from a parent:

- Are his senses and reflexes affected by certain medications or combinations of medications? If you notice a difference after he starts a new medication, check with his physician.

- Are medications or eye conditions interfering with her ability to focus or causing her to experience extra sensitivity to light, trouble seeing in the dark, or blurred vision?

- Is he driving closer and closer to traffic lights and street signs, slowing just to see the lights or signs?

- Can she react appropriately to drivers coming from behind or the side?

- Does he have decreased hearing? Can he heed emergency sirens or honking horns?

- Is your parent getting flustered while driving or quick to anger?

- Does your parent experience problems with memory? Does she miss exits that used to be second nature, or is she getting lost frequently?

- Do you see him making lane changes suddenly, drifting into other lanes, braking or accelerating suddenly?

- Does she fail to use her turn signal or keep the signal on without changing lanes?

- Has he had close calls and increased citations?

- Are there scrapes and dents on the car?

Cary's father-in-law, who was in his late eighties, refused to give up his license. Prior to his surrendering his license, Cary and Susie followed him home from dinner at a restaurant and watched him drift over the center line as he made a left turn. They also witnessed him driving through stop signs, because he felt they were "optional." These clues provided the information they needed to initiate the "giving-up-the-keys" discussion.

When the discussion started, Cary's father-in-law's arguments were: "I can still drive safely" and "I know what I can do, and you need to mind your own business." Both responses were defensive and contradicted the observations and the facts. Cary's response was, "Dad, we love you and we are concerned about your safety and Mom's. You should consider getting a driver to take you to your appointments, and we will drive you to dinners."

One strategy is to request that an older parent drive only during the day. This could be the first step to surrendering the license. Another strategy could be to have someone else in the family, someone they are more likely to listen to, speak with them. In Cary's case, his eldest nephew sat down with his grandparents and convinced them to use a driver. That began the process.

Finally, when Cary's father-in-law had an accident and his wife said she would not ride with him any longer, he stopped driving and surrendered the keys. Prior to giving up his keys, he purchased a replacement vehicle before the family saw the damage to the previous one. To say he was resistant to surrendering his license would be an understatement. His deteriorating eyesight, traffic violations, and the accident should have alerted Cary to initiate the conversation to pave the way to the ultimate surrender of his license. Ultimately, Susie's parents hired caregivers for household chores, and these individuals became the designated drivers and used the family vehicle to transport them.

In another situation, a close friend of Cary's got his mother to relent and give up her keys by discussing the financial impact of owning a car at her age. She refused initially but called him to pick up the car when she received the car insurance renewal bill. When confronted with the actual bill, she realized her son was right. She could no longer afford to own the car on her fixed income. Cary's friend now realizes that he could have done a better job of preparing his mother for this discussion.

A move to assisted living or a senior facility may also provide an opportunity to have the car keys conversation, especially if the facility provides transportation to doctor appointments, local entertainment, and shopping. Cary has been encouraging his friends whose parents are in their late eighties and early nineties to start the conversation, but it might be too late for them. The best outcomes will result from conversations held long before the surrender of the driver's license and car become necessary as result of ill health, an accident, or family finances.

A Parent Moving In

Many times it is not financially feasible for a parent to move into an assisted living or senior facility. One alternative is inviting your parent to move into your home. This option is fraught with challenges and potential pitfalls. The parent now becomes a member of your household, living under your roof, and involved with your daily routine. Your routine is going to be impacted by her presence and needs, including doctor appointments, medication, dietary restrictions, and activity schedules. If your children are still living at home, the situation may be even more complicated. You have your own approach to parenting, your dad or mom have their own parenting style, and you can expect to hear comments on what and how you discipline your children, and on other parent-child interactions.

Your first negotiation should be with your spouse when you become aware of the possibility of this arrangement. It is critical that you and your spouse are both ready to have another adult living in your home. Both spouses need to agree on how they will handle conflicts with the parent when they occur—and most likely they will. There will be concerns regarding privacy, meal selection, schedules, medical appointments, and other personal issues. It is possible that you and your spouse may not agree on a number of issues and a third party may be needed to work through these issues.

When the first negotiation is successfully completed with your spouse, the second negotiation should be with your parent. You cannot wait until your parent moves in to discuss potential conflicts; they need to be addressed prior to changing living arrangements. Topics to be discussed should include supporting your parenting approach, maintaining the family schedule, assisting with meals and other household chores, and use of the family vehicle. In cases where the parent requires assistance, you may need to plan for professional support. Physical changes to your home may be needed, for example, the installation of handicapped bars in the bathrooms, a ramp at the entrance, and/or other changes as required.

Reviewing a Will

Prior to your aging parent(s) entering a senior facility, assisted living, nursing home, or hospice care, you will need to need to discuss some very sensitive matters with them. Among these are the status of their wills and how they handle their finances.

If your parents do not have wills, it is important that they each have one drawn up by an attorney. Ideally, you or one of your siblings would be designated to follow through to make sure this actually happens. It is also going to become important to determine who will have the power of attorney so that you and your siblings will be prepared when the situation arises when a power of attorney is needed.

Wills can be simple or complex, depending on the number of siblings and the size of the estate. While many wills include an individual's desires regarding their funeral arrangements, others only address the distribution of assets, such as stocks, bonds, real estate, and furnishings. If the will does not include information about the burial wishes of your parent, we suggest that you separately address this topic with him or her, so that when your parent does pass away, you will be able to plan the funeral according to his or her wishes.

Because the number of family members can increase or decrease between the time when a will is first drafted and when it is enforced, encourage your parents to regularly review it, and when necessary, update the list of beneficiaries in their will—especially when there is a change in the family structure. This is extremely important if the will is going to be used to distribute assets, as the resulting discrepancies could contribute to interfamily conflicts and a need for probate. When a change is made to the will, it is important to contact an attorney, so the modified will can be properly filed.

In Cary's family, a cousin died unexpectedly. His mother was listed as the beneficiary on his teacher's pension plan. His mother, however, had predeceased him by over five years, and the court had to decide how to equitably distribute the assets among the first cousins. The concomitant expenses and the resulting conflicts among the cousins could have been prevented if the beneficiaries stated in the will and in other financial documents had been kept current.

With parents living longer and in better health, it becomes more challenging to have this conversation. Whether your parents reside with you or at their home, there will be times when they will need medical attention. If they are admitted to a hospital or the nursing home and are unable to make decisions regarding their own health, you will need a copy of their durable power of attorney.

Financial Matters

Talking with aging parents about their personal finances can be a difficult discussion, as your parents will most likely have strong personal feelings about this area. Be prepared for their initial resistance because you are intimating that they can no longer manage their own finances.

If the parents regularly use a checking and/or have a savings account, one or more of the children will need to be added to the checking and savings accounts so that funds can be accessed to pay their medical and personal expenses. Don't forget to find out if they are renting a safety deposit box at their local bank. (Usually the rental of safety deposit boxes is included in the monthly checking statements.)

In this day of electronic banking, adult children need to review with their elderly parents which expenses can be paid directly and electronically. When Cary initiated such a discussion with his father-in-law about the household finances, he immediately experienced substantial push-back. It took several lengthy discussions before his father-in-law shared the passwords and user names for recurring monthly payments and their investment accounts. This information was critical to maintaining the household for his wife after he passed away.

During a review of their parents' household expenses, one of the Cary's closest friends discovered that her father was making regular donations to nonprofit organizations that had solicited him by direct mail. Upon investigation, she discovered that many of these organizations were not as advertised and delivered little or no money to their clients. It is known that these types of organizations directly market to seniors because they are seen as easy marks. She immediately discontinued those payments even though she received resistance from her father. The source of this resistance was the perceived "loss of control" over his finances.

The use of facts is the suggested power selection in these types of negotiations. You may require the assistance of the parents' accountant or attorney to support your actions. If they continue to resist, you may need to obtain power of attorney so you can gain access to their account information with their bank and other financial institutions.

After the death of his father-in-law, Cary was able to access his personal computer and review his over 4,500 emails. Cary closed accounts, cancelled credit cards, cancelled some automatic payments, and converted other automatic payments into invoices so his mother-in-law could write monthly checks as long as she still maintained her checkbook.

As in many circumstances, the surviving spouse in a pre-boomer-generation marriage has little or no knowledge of the Internet or how to operate a computer or access emails and other types of electronic correspondence. In these instances, they would require the support and assistance of their children or grandchildren in managing their finances.

Moving to Assisted Living or a Senior Facility

Prior to talking with your parent(s) about moving from their current home to a senior facility, assisted living, or nursing home, siblings need to agree among themselves about the type of living arrangement they think would be best for their parents. Many times there will be resistance from the parents about leaving their home, and if one or more siblings align with their parents, it could delay or even derail the move to a senior or assisted living facility.

It is very important to anticipate situations that will require negotiating a change in lifestyle for a parent or loved one. It is suggested that site visits be set up in advance so the parents can see how many options there are and how other seniors, especially their peers, are dealing with the move to a senior facility or assisted living. These early site visits permit the parents to choose where they desire to spend their senior years, rather than the situation Cary faced with his mother.

Many years ago Cary's mother had stomach surgery at age eighty-five to remove a malignant tumor. After she recovered and left the hospital, she returned to her one-bedroom apartment, which she had occupied for over fifty years in the borough of Queens in New York. After she was settled with her caregiver, Cary and his brother had a conversation about what would happen next. Cary's brother agreed that their mother should stay in the apartment until she could no longer take care of herself. Then Cary sat down with his mother and explained his and his brother's position. She agreed with their assessment of the situation.

Six years later Cary received a call at five in the morning from his brother on New Year's Day stating that their mother called him after she flooded the kitchen. A friend of Cary's brother came over, assessed the situation, and reported that their mother was somewhat disoriented and very agitated. Cary called her later that morning and reminded her of their previous discussion regarding an assisted living facility. She remembered and said she understood that she needed to move into a more controlled situation. Cary's brother drove to New York the next week and took their mother on a tour of assisted living facilities near his home in the Pittsburgh area. She selected one location and moved in a week later. Cary flew to New York the next weekend and the two sons packed up their childhood belongings and reminisced about their childhood over a glass of scotch as they closed her apartment.

So why did this negotiation and transition go so smoothly? The answer lies in the fact that Cary and his brother anticipated the need to make the move and negotiated with their mother while she was still cognitively intact and could make an informed decision. Because the decision was not imminent, she felt less defensive about it. When the decision needed to be implemented, there was some initial resistance to giving up her home of so many years, but their mother was a realist and relented.

There was little or no conflict because Cary and his brother agreed upon their strategy prior to speaking with their mother. In this manner, she had no opportunity to play one brother against the other or create an alliance that would defend her position. The brothers approached the situation with a united front: she would need to move when she could no longer take care of herself. Since both of them lived hours away from New York, they could not provide the daily support she required.

The moral of this story is that preplanning works and so does preparing the parent for a change in her lifestyle and providing sufficient time to adjust to change. No one likes change, especially when it is thrust upon them.

Last Wishes

Some seniors have preplanned every detail of their funeral, while others have done no preplanning at all. When you become aware that your parents have not done any preplanning, you need to respond in a timely manner. The first question you should ask a parent is where a copy of their will is located. If the answer is that there is no will, you have another challenge ahead of you. (See the section "Reviewing a Will" earlier in this chapter for guidance.) Even if your parent has a will that includes his wishes regarding his funeral, it is helpful to have a conversation about how the parent would like to be remembered, the funeral service, and where he would like to be buried.

In the case where your parents have preplanned the service and purchased cemetery plots, you need to ensure that these documents are secured in a safety deposit box or at an attorney's office. Check that they were properly prepared by an attorney and are updated as needed to reflect the current state of their financial affairs.

In some cases, older adults have not purchased a final resting place or made any arrangements with a funeral director. This can be a challenging situation for the survivors. Decisions will be impacted by the availability or cost of the plot, the casket, and the ceremony. Since no instructions were left in writing, you are only relying on the memory of previous conversations with your parents and your siblings. Perhaps you have nothing to rely on and have to make many decisions quickly.

There is a need to achieve consensus among the surviving spouse and the adult children. The initial conversation should take place with the surviving spouse, who will share not only her wishes but those of her life partner. What emanates from this discussion will serve as the foundation for the funeral. For the funerals of both Cary's mother and mother-in-law, the stated wishes were that they wanted the same funeral as their spouse. Even the service construct and content were very similar. The real negotiation here was with the siblings and the funeral director to ensure that the deceased's wishes are respected.

A dear friend of Cary's had both of his in-laws in the same hospital at the same time. The wife was dying of cancer and the husband was hospitalized for prostate cancer. The husband met with his son-in-law and stated that his wife changed her mind regarding who would oversee her funeral. He reported that she insisted that a particular rabbi not perform the service and that his assistant do it. Here the wishes were communicated through a son-in-law instead of a son or daughter, and the son-in-law had to implement the mother-in-law's wishes, even if the other children did not agree. This could have been a contentious situation, but because they were her last wishes, there was no negotiation. The rest of her family and her two sons had no choice but to trust that their brother-in-law got it right.

When Cary's father-in-law died, his wife thought that there was only one life insurance policy. A careful examination of his personal papers revealed that there were five other policies with the same insurance company. He had never shared that fact with his wife. The policies were not in a safety deposit box but instead were buried among his personal papers. These situations can be avoided with an open and honest discussion among the parents and their children prior to the onset of a disease or old age.

It is not always the oldest child who is the best choice to discuss these matters with the parents; it might not even be a child at all. In some cases it could be a trusted contemporary, such as a dear friend, business advisor, member of the clergy, or attorney. These issues have to be discussed and resolved.

Splitting Up the Household Possessions

After your parents have passed away, there may be household items, jewelry, artwork, pictures, and other personal items that need to be shared among family members. There is a good chance that most of these items have been omitted from your parents' wills. This situation has many potential pitfalls and opportunities for conflict. Each sibling, grandchild, and great grand-child could have an emotional connection to a specific item. This connection should be acknowledged, and each person should be permitted to take possession of such an item. Whether it is a picture, a piece of furniture, china, or some other item, the emotional connection runs deep and could cause conflict if ignored.

The siblings must meet and determine how these items will be distributed. After Cary's in-laws passed, he and his wife sat down with the family, including the grandchildren, and discussed how this challenge would be managed. Susie, her sister, and the sons of one sister who had predeceased their grandparents, made their choices first. After they made their choices, it was determined that the great-grandchildren would use colored stickers to identify the items they wanted to take home to remember their grandparents. When two of them wanted the same knick-knack, they were left to work it out their own. If there was conflict, it needed to be negotiated. Items were traded until both parties felt satisfied.

The balance of the furniture and furnishings were donated to a local charity. Cary had arranged with that charity to provide a truck and two men to assist in loading the furnishings. Some items went into storage until they could be properly prepared for shipping to the designated recipients.

Lessons Learned

- Prior to discussions and negotiations with your older adult parents, engage the assistance of their physicians, social workers, attorneys, and other influential people in their lives.

- Older adults view the ability to drive and own a car as a sign of independence. This very sensitive topic needs to be raised by the adult children when they feel that their parent or parents no longer can drive safely. You can't wait for an accident or major traffic violation to act. Be prepared to expect significant resistance from your parent.

- When you become aware of the potential for a parent to move into your home, your first negotiation should be with your spouse. Both spouses must agree on how they will handle conflicts when they inevitably occur with the parent. It is possible that the spouses may not agree on a number of issues and a third party may be needed to work through these issues.

- As your parents age, it is important to have a discussion with them regarding the status of their wills, and to confirm that they, in fact, have wills. The list of beneficiaries in a will should be reviewed regularly, especially when there is a change in the family structure. Any changes in a will should be properly filed with an attorney. Similarly, it is important to make sure that your parents have designated a power of attorney.

- Another sensitive discussion that has to take place is regarding household expenses and how they are managed. If the parents use a regular checking and/or savings account, one or more of the children will need to be added to those accounts so that funds can be accessed to pay the parents' medical and personal expenses. Where appropriate, the children will need to obtain the necessary power of attorney documents from the family attorney to act on behalf of their parents.

- It is important to anticipate the need to move your parent(s) to a senior or assisted living facility. This negotiation should take place with your parents while they are still cognitively intact and can make an informed decision. Prior to talking with your parents, siblings should agree among themselves about the type of living arrangement they think would be best for their parents. Many times parents may resist the idea of giving up their home, and if one or more siblings align with their parents, it could derail the move.

(continued)

- Speak with your parents about their last wishes and their preferred funeral arrangements, as these are sensitive topics that should not be ignored. You may need to select a family member, trusted friend, or advisor who can review these issues with your parent or parents so their wishes can be honored. Having clarity about these topics early on will prevent potential conflict among the siblings at the time of the funeral.

CHAPTER TEN

Dealing with Healthcare Professionals, Insurance Companies, and Friends

Dan has had recurring back pains for months, and his family is encouraging him to see an orthopedist for an evaluation. After having a MRI and other tests, the doctor determines that Dan has two discs that need to be fused in order for him to alleviate the pain and other symptoms. This doctor has "expert power," as he was highly recommended and has years of experience in his field. Dan is reluctant to challenge his course of treatment. After consulting with his two sons and their wives, one of whom is a surgical nurse, Dan seeks out a second opinion and elects a less invasive procedure, which proves effective.

This chapter addresses situations in which you normally find yourself uncomfortable negotiating—those involving a healthcare professional or healthcare provider or friends. We will share real-life situations where we and some of our family members negotiated with a healthcare provider on behalf of themselves or a parent. We also address the challenges of interacting with "toxic" friends and provide strategies for dealing with them in a healthy manner.

Negotiating with Healthcare Professionals
As a young child, Cary remembers hearing his mother say more than once, "Listen to your doctor." It is not unusual for you to feel a lack of control when you are dealing with your doctor, dentist, or other health providers,

because for years you have been told they know best. Many of those health professionals, as well, have approached patients with an authoritarian "doctor-knows-best" style. Today, with the advent of the Internet, especially websites such as WebMD.com, we are more informed than ever regarding symptoms, medications, treatments, tests, and medical procedures.

Furthermore, many physicians are now employees of healthcare systems that are especially interested in making sure patients are satisfied with their care. Healthcare systems now routinely send out surveys asking patients to rate their doctors on everything from timeliness to listening skills. What many patients don't know is that such ratings are used to determine physicians' salaries. Healthcare providers now have a monetary incentive to listen to patients, and to be open and collaborate about their care. Authoritarian physicians don't fare well on such surveys.

The relationship between physicians and patients is undergoing major changes, and patients have an opportunity to benefit from this evolution. It is also true that many healthcare professionals, as employees of major healthcare systems, are rewarded for making fewer referrals. As the patient, this requires you to advocate for yourself and negotiate with your healthcare professional to receive the care you need.

In today's medical marketplace, many of the larger medical practices put the emphasis on productivity, not the patient. We have heard more than one friend state that they felt the doctor did not spend sufficient time with them discussing their case. This is not the patient-focused approach we and our parents experienced in the later part of the twentieth century. Today you are greeted by the medical assistant, ushered into the examining room, your vitals are taken, and then you are examined by the physician's assistant (PA) or nurse practitioner (NP). In some cases, the doctor will actually examine you and discuss your case. In other instances, you may need to negotiate with the PA and state that you have a concern about your symptoms and would like to talk to the doctor. You should articulate that you have confidence in what they have said, but if it's not possible to speak with your doctor during this visit, can they assist you in making another appointment so you can talk with your doctor.

As patients, we perceive that these professionals possess legitimate, information, and some expert power due to their knowledge and experience in their chosen fields. When entering into a discussion with a healthcare professional—a doctor, dentist, psychologist and even a nurse—unless you are incapacitated, you are your own best advocate. One night while Cary was having dinner with his in-laws and wife at a local restaurant, he passed out at the table. When he awoke, the paramedics were there and suggested that Cary go to the hospital for evaluation. He refused their offer to be transported and released them. Both his wife and his in-laws insisted he go to the emergency department at the nearby hospital, and eventually Cary relented. He was admitted to the hospital after being diagnosed with atrial fibrillation by the cardiology resident on duty.

The next morning the hospitalist on the cardiac floor visited Cary and suggested that an MRI scan be performed. The discussion/negotiation began by Cary asking why it was necessary. The hospitalist responded by stating that according to the admitting form, Cary had fallen and passed out, and the hospitalist felt it necessary to rule out any possibility of a stroke. Cary informed him that the initial diagnosis was atrial fibrillation and not a stroke and that the scan was not needed. The hospitalist pressed his point using the legitimate power he possessed as a physician. Cary responded that he would need to discuss his request with his cardiologist and base the decision on the cardiologist's expert opinion. There was no compromise; it was the cardiologist's expert power versus his legitimate power. Cary's cardiologist agreed that the scan was not necessary based on Cary's medical history, lab tests, and the cardiologist's examination. In this situation, Cary did not compromise; he used information power and the expert power of his cardiologist, and he prevailed. The moral here is that the doctor is not always right.

In another medical battle of the wills, Cary's father-in-law was admitted to the hospital with congestive heart failure. At the time he was admitted, Cary and Susie were out of town but flew back to Milwaukee upon hearing of his hospitalization.

Upon their arrival, Cary and Susie found her father depressed, with no appetite, withdrawn, and very reclusive. After speaking with their family, especially Susie's mother, they realized that Susie's father thought he was dying, and he had given up. His decision was based on conversations he had overheard among the doctors about his condition. Again Cary found himself dealing with a hospitalist who had very little knowledge of the patient's personality and psychological history. Cary requested a psychological work-up by the hospital's psychiatrist to evaluate and document his father-in-law's mental state. The psychiatrist's evaluation was that the patient was suffering from depression because he was upset about being in the hospital and not in his home.

The family could have accepted the diagnosis, but since Cary had experience in the behavioral sciences and was knowledgeable regarding his father-in-law's behavioral patterns, he disagreed with the diagnosis and elected to consult with another expert. By using expert and referent power, which is defined by whom you know, Cary was able to engage the resident psychiatrist in a dialogue that resulted in the administration of an antidepressant to his father-in-law. He regained his appetite, and his level of interpersonal interaction increased. As a result of his improved demeanor and physical condition, he was able to transition to a rehabilitation facility, where he lived in a reasonable level of comfort for an additional eight months.

Cary could have accepted the doctor's initial diagnosis but chose to negotiate on behalf of his father-in-law and act as his advocate. In the previous case, Cary advocated for himself; in this case, he advocated for another individual. You can successfully negotiate with healthcare professionals if you correctly use information as well as expert and referent power.

End-of-life Issues

Due to the highly competitive world of healthcare today, providers and healthcare systems are more willing to consider the perspective of patients and their loved ones and are reluctant to alienate the public. Often there is no negotiation with the doctor when addressing end-of-life issues. However, because of recent changes in the law regarding end-of-life issues, in a number of states, namely Oregon, Washington, Vermont, Montana and California, patients may elect to end their life at a time they feel is medically appropriate.

In many cases, the doctor will recognize that the patient is in such decline that they counsel the patient and the family to consider palliative care, which focuses on relieving symptoms and improving quality of life. This level of care is provided either in the patient's home or at a hospice. This involves a multi-level negotiation, between the doctor and the patient, and the doctor and the immediate family. The patient's wishes need to be honored by the family along with the expert information provided by the doctor.

Cary's mother-in-law was repeatedly treated at the local emergency room for the same diagnosis. Over time, her ability to swallow deteriorated, affecting her lungs. Her doctor suggested home hospice, which provides care for terminally ill patients but no treatment for their under-lying medical condition. The doctor asked the family to step out of the room; he presented his diagnosis to her and suggested that she strongly consider home hospice care. Cary's mother-in-law agreed based on the information the doctor provided plus his expertise, and she began to receive palliative care in her home. She passed quietly five days later.

Negotiating with Insurance Companies

In this section, we address your discussions/negotiations with healthcare providers as they relate to your dealings with insurance companies. How many times has each of us heard from the pharmacist that the insurance company wishes to substitute a generic or another drug for the one pre-scribed by our doctor? Many people feel that if they wish to continue with the drug of choice, they must pay for it. The answer is both yes and no. Yes, you may have to pay a higher amount for the specified prescription, and no, if your doctor can convince the insurance company that this is the drug that best fits your specific needs.

On more than one occasion, Cary has successfully negotiated with an insurance company in order to retain a drug or his wife's medication of choice. Cary did so by using expert and information power, and the powers provided to him by his doctor. In one instance, it was a drug for choles-terol; another time it was a drug for acid reflux. Both times the doctor specified that the drug the insurance company suggested would not be the best solution for the medical condition. You need to convince the insurance company by using information power and expert power that your case is unique and that a "cookie cutter" solution will not be the best resolution for your problem. Many healthcare providers and hospital systems have patient advocates available if the negotiation breaks down.

Another mechanism is available—an appeal process provided by the insurance company for their subscribers. In this process, you need to incorporate both information power and expert power to present the facts that support your request for the specific treatment or medication required to maintain your health. Recently, for example, the insurance company declined to cover a drug prescribed for Cary's wife. They felt it was a duplicate and not required as part of her formulary. It took two negotiations by Cary and a letter from the prescribing doctor pointing out the risks involved to his wife's long-term health in not providing the drug to get them to relent and approve it.

As part of the process, you need to point out any downside risks to the insurer if the treatment or drug is not approved. These include the declining health or potential death of the patient, which could result in a claim of negligence against the insurance company. If your life or that of your partner could be put at risk without the prescribed drug or treatment, the insurance company has no choice but to reconsider their decision.

Again we are speaking about advocacy, both on your part and the part of the doctor. As an individual, with the assistance of your doctor, you can successfully negotiate with your insurance company and get the treatments and prescriptions you require to maintain your health.

Dealing with Toxic Friends

We all have friends who could be defined as "toxic": they talk only about themselves, impose their problems on you, and are overly critical about everything. These people need to be removed from your circle of friends. Fox News in Houston featured a segment on June 19, 2014, on "The five warning signs of a toxic relationship and five ways to end one," created by reporter Alexander Supgul. The identifiers he suggested are:

- They are openly critical of you.

- They talk negatively of other people you care about.

- They take advantage of you emotionally and financially.

- They criticize your feelings.

- They make you feel you are the only person they trust.

In a January 26, 2006, article posted by Heather Hatfield on WEBMD, professor Charles Figly, PhD, of Florida State University found that you continue a relationship with a toxic friend because:

- You feel trapped in the relationship.

- She makes you feel that she has no one else to turn to.

A common question the authors have been presented with is, "How do you deal with such people?" In many cases, you cannot negotiate with them. One answer lies in establishing boundaries and enforcing them.

According to the Fox News Houston segment, "The only way to get out of the relationship is to distance yourself from them" [toxic people]. You don't need to be in these one-sided relationships. Toxic friends will suck you emotionally dry. Here are five strategies they suggest you use to end a toxic relationship:

1. Stop making excuses for your toxic friends. It's time to let them go when they step over the boundaries by disrespecting you, or by making you feel bad. You can try to negotiate by stating, "I will have no choice but to end the friendship unless you begin treating me with respect."

2. It is normal to give people a "second chance" but set boundaries for the friendship. For example, inform her that you will not take calls after a set time or that you want to limit the number of calls to you in a day.

3. Maintain your focus on your life, not on their problems. A toxic friend can leave you feeling unmotivated by leaching and sucking out your energy. Keep the calls brief and hang up when she is beginning to affect

your energy. Phrases that will get you off the phone are, "I need to go" or "Someone is at the door."

4. Reveal your feelings about your toxic friends with your non-toxic, real friends. They can be a source of comfort to you. They will be there to support you when you decide to extract yourself from these unhealthy relationships. They may also serve as a source of strategies that could assist in ending toxic relationships.

5. Be honest with your toxic friends and let them know how you really feel. It is difficult to tell someone how we truly feel about the relationship. Using statements like, "I feel sad after every time we talk" or "Our conversations are draining" will signal that you are not comfortable with the status of the relationship.

Be aware that toxic friends may ignore many of your attempts to end the relationship. They are so focused on their needs that they are not processing that you are unhappy. You must stress the fact that you need to discontinue the relationship unless their behavior changes. In many cases, they will not hear you and continue to be toxic. Toxic people will not take any responsibility for the toxic relationship and blame others for the change in its status. You then have to make a decision to continue as is or take the necessary steps to exit the relationship.

Lessons Learned

- You can negotiate with your healthcare provider and your insurance company regarding medications prescribed and treatment options. You need to advocate for yourself and assemble information from your doctor and other experts that supports your request and provides the power you need to achieve your objectives. In addition, ask your doctor to advocate for you with the insurance company during the appeal process to ensure you get the care you need.

- You as an individual can act as an advocate for yourself and others by negotiating the level of care with the attending healthcare professionals; this includes nurse practitioners and physician assistants. The doctor is not always right, and you need to be aware of your options as a patient. You need to be informed and not be afraid to request a second or even a third opinion—invite other experts into the conversation.

- When it comes to end-of-life issues, there should be no negotiation. The wishes of the individual should be respected by both the doctor and the family.

- There is nothing wrong with setting boundaries when dealing with friends, especially toxic ones. If they cannot respect your wishes and are intrusive, they should not be your friends.

- You need to be aware when toxic friends become intrusive, disruptive, and insensitive to your feelings. You need to ask yourself the question, "Is this friendship one of value?" If the answer is no, then you should terminate the relationship.

CHAPTER ELEVEN

Negotiating in a Business Setting

Jon, who has just graduated with a degree in accounting, has an interview with a national public accounting firm. Jon has interned with a local accounting firm for the last four years but desires to work for a national firm. He has developed his resume with the assistance of the school's placement office, but has no formal training in how to interview and negotiate a salary or benefits. Jon is very nervous about this important interview. What should be his next step?

I t is obvious that Jon needs to prepare for this upcoming interview and salary negotiation. His best strategy is to do his homework and establish baselines for starting salaries and benefits for first-year accountants. Jon should leverage his four years of experience (information power) to support a request for a higher starting salary.

Jon also needs to be aware that business-oriented negotiations differ greatly from those with family, personal, and social relationships. In business negotiations, you are expected to make decisions within tight time frames and with little or no chance to collect in-depth information. Also, the emotional connection is lower for a negotiation in a business relationship than it is in a personal one. In some business scenarios, your reputation may be on the line, which adds to the increase in the stress and intensity of the negotiation.

There are power relationships within business negotiations that need to be considered. Your boss and his bosses have legitimate power and referent power. Initially you will need to rely on information as your only source of power. As you build your expertise, you will develop expert power. Negative sources of power, such as coercive behavior and even threats, may be used in a negotiation by your peers and bosses. You will need to anticipate such uses of power by your negotiating counterparts.

We will look at various scenarios, including Jon negotiating his first job, the performance appraisal, dealing with suppliers and customers, and coping with the office bully.

Your First Job

As a young child, Cary needed to find a way to earn money to support his growing bubble gum habit. He went from store to store on 35th Avenue in Jackson Heights, Queens, New York, asking proprietors if they needed someone to sweep floors, shovel snow, deliver groceries, or stock shelves. After a number of negative responses, he received a positive one, and began to stock the shelves at a locally owned pharmacy. No interview, no resume, no pre-employment drug testing, no background check. Things were just that simple in the 1950s.

In today's competitive world, finding and then negotiating the terms of your first job is not that simple. After graduation from college and graduate school, the newly minted BA or MBA has to find an organization in which he can apply what he learned over the past sixteen to eighteen years. If the university/college does not have a strong placement office or does not encourage on-campus recruiting, the graduate heads for the computer lab and signs on to the Internet to begin his search for employment opportunities. In some cases, he has had jobs or internships during the summers and has already started to build a resume and search network.

Many graduates enter the marketplace with little or no employment background relative to the position they are seeking. However, having interviewed hundreds of recent graduates throughout his career, Cary has found numerous graduates who were focused on their career path and elected to intern or work in their field or related areas prior to graduation. This permitted them to build their network, expertise, and resumes. These students come into an interview armed with knowledge of the industry, experience, and the skill sets desired by the employer. Unless they are totally introverted and nonverbal, they have a head start on the competition.

So what are the steps necessary for Jon to prepare for that all-important interview and salary negotiation?

1. Prepare an updated resume for the desired position, using the job description as your focus. For each cover letter and resume that you submit, match your skills to those outlined in the job description or job posting. Whenever possible list quantifiable results under each job achievement.

2. Use the Internet to research the company, its management, its competition, and its position in the marketplace. This information will serve you well during the interview process.

3. Research salaries and benefits in your area for the same or comparable positions at similar companies. There are a number of government and public websites that contain these statistics. For example www.DOL. gov contains data on wages and benefits. This permits you to develop information power for your salary negotiation.

4. Develop a budget so you can determine how much money you really need to cover your rent, food, insurance (health, home, and auto) and other expenses in that geographical location. This basic level of salary will be your **WATNA**, which is your **W**orst **A**lternative **T**o a **N**egotiated **A**greement (see Chapter Two). It is the salary number you do not want to accept.

5. Determine the salary range and benefits that you can accept, which would be reflected in your **ZOPA** —your **Z**one **O**f **P**otential Agreement (also discussed in Chapter Two). Any offer that falls within this zone would be a "win."

6. It is not in your best interest for your first interview to be with the company you desire the most. If you can, set up one or more interviews with your second- and third-tier companies to gather information and build your confidence and interviewing skills.

7. After interviewing with the second- and third-tier companies, you now have developed one or more of your **BATNA**s, which are your **B**est **A**lternatives **T**o a **N**egotiated **A**greement. Should you not get the first-tier position, you may have two other valid offers to accept. Those offers also provide some guidance about salary possibilities and provide the opportunity for you to experience one or more salary negotiations.

Once Jon has gained experience, information, and insights from his previous interviews, he is ready for the "major leagues." Now he has a better understanding of the process, and has gathered information about salary ranges and benefits. He has also gained experience including his skill sets in his presentation. In addition, these interactions have increased his self-confidence.

The Interview

It is rare that you have the edge in a job interview unless you have skills that are unique, valuable, and desired by the company conducting the interview. Normally you are competing with a number of candidates with similar qualifications. So how do you stand out from the crowd? Your resume, which Cary calls the "silent interview," is the key that opens the door to the interview. As stated earlier, it should be targeted to the particular job you are applying for and not be generic in its content; ditto for the cover letter. You always want to match your skill set to the ones outlined in the published job description or posting.

Once you have been contacted by the company conducting the interviews, your negotiation preparation begins. By now, you have completed steps one through seven and are ready to participate in the interview process and the eventual salary and benefit negotiation. When the interview begins, don't be afraid to ask questions if you require clarification regarding job duties, training, company culture, 401(k), or benefits. Stay away from discussing vacation and retirement benefits. Your focus should be on getting started, not taking time off or retiring. You would be surprised at the number of applicants who inquire about time off and retirement benefits even before they are offered the job. This does not play well with the interviewer.

During the interview, feel free to ask questions about the company's markets and products and how it conducts business. These types of questions demonstrate you are really interested in the company. Because you have had a number of previous interviews, you should be relaxed and understand how the process works. In some circumstances, you may receive a tour of the facility, be interviewed by more than one manager, and be taken to lunch. Be aware that each individual you interact with is part of the interviewing process and is evaluating you. At the end of the interview process, each individual who interacted with you will submit an evaluation of their interactions with you to Human Resources. It is a good idea to follow up the interview with a thank-you note.

The Offer

It is possible during the interview that there will be no discussion of salary or benefits. They will focus on your experience, your skills, your answers to their questions and scenarios, and your overall attitude. After they review your interview results, the evaluations of the other individuals who interacted with you, and the evaluations of the other candidates, they will begin the ranking process. An offer will go to the top candidate first, and if it is not you, you will receive a thank-you letter. If you are the top candidate, you will either be asked to come in for a follow-up interview or be offered the position on the telephone. If it is a telephone offer, you could be at a disadvantage, because you cannot read body language or the facial expressions of the person on the telephone. If the offer is made by phone, you should follow these guidelines:

1. Let the company representative speak first and make the job offer. This offer should include an initial salary and a starting date of employment.

2. Clarify whether this is a starting salary subject to review after some specific period of time or an annual salary.

3. Based on your previous interviews, does this salary offer fit into your ZOPA per your budgetary requirements? If not, you need to counter the offer at this time.

4. Present your counter offer in a "neutral" manner. For example, you may say, "Based upon my budget, I require this level of salary to be able to live in your location." You could be more direct and state with confidence (because you have an offer from another firm, your BATNA) that you have been offered a higher salary from another company. If they really want you, they will match or exceed the other offer. Be prepared for the possibility that they might tell you to take the other offer.

5. Before accepting the offer you need to monetize the benefits (that is, assign a dollar value to them) and add them to the salary offered to determine the value of the total package.

6. Don't forget to discuss relocation expenses. Some companies will pay or contribute to your costs of moving and put you up in temporary housing until you find a permanent home. Be aware that these contributions will show up in your annual income summary (W-2). You will then need to itemize these relocation expenses in your income taxes for that year.

7. If the job offer requires relocation outside the United States for training or orientation, ask who will arrange for the necessary visas and complete the required paperwork with the State Department. Inquire if there are any other requirements that have to be met, inoculations, for example.

8. If they don't specify benefits, ask which benefits are available to new hires. Some companies have "cafeteria benefits," which permit you to choose among a variety of benefits. You don't need to make your choices at this time. These decisions will come later when your paperwork is being processed by Human Resources.

9. If you are considering their final offer, thank them and inquire when they need an answer and what would be the next steps in the process. The negotiation is over once the interview is concluded and you accept the offer, so it is important to have some time to digest and evaluate their final offer.

10. You have one step left. You need to contact the other companies by phone or email that made you an offer. Thank them and inform them that you have accepted another offer. You want to close those negotiations on a positive note. You may receive another offer from these companies in the future, so keep the door open.

In order to recruit you, many companies will offer to assist your wife, husband, or partner in finding a position. This is a topic that should be raised early in the interview and should be included in the negotiation process. For example, many hospitals that actively recruit physicians will provide assistance in finding a position for the wife, husband, or partner. Many of these physicians are married, in some instances to another physician. The recruiting hospital will either find the second physician a position in their facility or with a local practice. They see this as part of their recruiting process, and in many cases, it could be a "deal breaker" if they cannot relocate the other person in the relationship.

The Performance Appraisal

Just the thought of preparing and executing an annual performance appraisal sends chills down the spine of many a senior manager and strikes fear into the employee. Performance appraisals are—at least they should be—nothing more than a collaborative conversation between individuals about opportunities to increase an individual's skill sets and value to the employer. The keys to a successful conversation in a performance negotiation lie in detailed preparation and the ability for both parties to communicate the importance of maintaining or improving performance. These conversations should be scheduled on a timely basis, generally yearly, but sooner if there are performance problems.

Any performance appraisal discussion should include a self-appraisal component. This component of the process is designed to increase the amount of communication between the appraiser and the person being evaluated. This interaction between the parties permits the person being appraised to rate his own performance and create the basis for a dialogue. The appraiser can then respond to each point outlined, and both parties can agree on the rating, agree to disagree, or amend the rating after a full discussion of each other's perceptions.

In many ways, a performance appraisal is, in fact, a negotiation. When the parties "agree to disagree," it is a result of an interactive discussion where neither party can convince the other to agree to a rating. In fact, there is a "perceptual gap" in which one person sees it one way and the other sees it differently. Here is an opportunity to use the information power we referred to Chapter Two. If you can support your perception with facts and figures, and the other person in the discussion cannot refute your facts, then she must relent and adopt your perception of the situation. The same goes for when you cannot refute her perception of your performance in a particular area of responsibility.

Another area where you can apply negotiation principles is in the setting of goals, both performance and personal, for the next calendar year. You—as a supervisor, manager, or employee—have the right to contribute to this section of the performance appraisal. You will be held accountable for the achievement of these goals, so you need to shape them in a fashion that will permit you to achieve them in a timely manner. These goals should be **SMART** goals, which means they are **S**pecific, **M**easurable, **A**chievable, **R**ealistic, and **T**imely (see Chapter One). The more quantitative the goal, the easier it is to measure. Qualitative goals, on the other hand, are more open to discussion and interpretation and can lead to conflict over their achievement.

The goal of a performance appraisal is to have a collaborative conversation. As the employee, you should leave the appraisal session feeling that you contributed and you were heard. You need to prepare for this appraisal session as if it were a negotiation and assemble any information that will support your self-evaluation. Both parties also have an opportunity to buy into performance goals they helped craft. In this way, it becomes a collaborative conversation, not a one-way lecture. This approach has a positive impact on performance and builds a relationship between the parties as well as an open communication channel. By being fully prepared, you have the opportunity to make your next performance appraisal conference a positive experience.

Finding Common Ground

As stated in earlier chapters, you need to find "common ground" in any negotiation. By using the "two-column approach" described in Chapter Two and listing each individual's interests, you will discover the common ground from which you can launch your negotiation. It will also be helpful to identify potential areas of disagreement. Through this process, you might also discover why your negotiation counterpart has taken a specific position with regard to one or more particular interests. Using all of this information, you can begin to build a foundation for current and future creative solutions.

In order to arrive at "win-win" collaborative solutions, each party in the negotiation must keep an open mind by considering new and creative solutions developed during the search for common ground. They also need to understand the other side's interests, the source of their power, and any possible reasons they would not agree to a proposed solution.

We must recognize that there are times when issues cannot be resolved. Both sides have defendable positions. Shall we proceed with another item of interest or adjourn? The choice is up to all the parties involved in the negotiation. One way to move past the impasse and proceed is to move to another item on the agenda. It is always good idea to start with a common interest and build from there. This will work when the negotiators can agree to agenda items one by one. The problem is sometimes it is an all-or-nothing negotiation.

As negotiators, our goal is to be respected and effective. Being liked or accepted should hold little value and be secondary. The key is to maintain your emotional control and remain nurturing enough to keep the other party engaged in the conversation. While it may feel good to punch the bully in the mouth at the table, you will need to be ready to let the deal go. Always let the adversary save face. You never know when you will need to deal with him in the future.

Dealing with Different Leadership Styles

To be successful in business, you need to be aware of and learn how to work with—or at least adapt to—the particular leadership style of your superior. It can be even a greater challenge in a family business, when your "boss" could be your parent, sibling, or other relative. Being aware of the leadership style of your surperior and learning how to best deal with that kind of personality can be extremely beneficial and can help you to avoid a lot of conflict. Knowledge of your boss's leadership style will also guide you in figuring out the best way to negotiate with him or her. Below are two extremes in leadership styles along with our suggestions for dealing with each.

The dictatorial/autocratic leader. Cary worked for a dictatorial/auto-cratic leader who did not easily welcome input from his management team or employees, and kept a tight grip on all areas of the company. The organizational chart was a "wagon wheel," with all major decisions being routed through the president's office. This slowed the decision-making process. The company president was rarely open to suggestions from his management team and continued to manage the business the same way he had done when the company had one-tenth of its current volume. In most cases, recommendations were not approved unless they supported his vision for the direction of the company. This type of micro-management approach will eventually strangle a business, thwart its growth, and could lead to the company's demise.

The only way to deal with such a control-oriented personality is to "play by the rules" until you gain his trust and confidence. It took more than a year for Cary to gain the needed respect and trust to be able to be part of the decision-making process. There were many times Cary and the owner disagreed. Cary stood his ground, however, and used "information power" and "expert power" to convince the owner that the recommenda-tions were in the best interest of the company. When proposing a solution to the owner about an existing problem, Cary used information power, arming himself with facts. Cary knew that the owner's primary focus was on generating the largest profit possible, so he would always identify the savings or the avoidance of cost in his proposals to gain the owner's support and approval.

The inclusive leader. This type of leader encourages input from her senior employees or management team and respects each individual's opinion. She strives to build consensus and is open to input from the staff. Communication is two way, unlike with a dictatorial leader. As employees demonstrate proficiency, they are given additional challenges and decision-making responsibility. Employees that show promise are mentored by senior staff (or by the owner herself) and are groomed to successfully assume future roles in the organization.

Dealing with the inclusive leader is much easier than working with the "dictator." The road to inclusion is smoother. The inclusive leader will give her management team opportunities to demonstrate that they can make informed decisions and lead their subordinates in the achievement of their assigned tasks. Once again, information power works best when negotiating with this type of leader.

No matter the personality of the owner of a company, communication is a key component for continued success in any negotiation scenario. But remember, in most cases changes need to be negotiated in small increments.

Negotiating with Your Boss

A major challenge to your negotiating skills is when you need to negotiate with your manager or supervisor. Typical negotiation scenarios involve the time and talent required to perform a task, financial resources to complete an assignment, additional responsibility, and an increased level of compensation.

Cary was in the retail business as a buyer when he regularly negotiated with his merchandise manager for more floor space, sales support, additional funding for advertising money, and higher inventory levels. In these types of negotiations, you need to come armed with information (information power) that will support your requests, knowing that your boss has both legitimate power based on his position in the company and economic power, because he controls the dollars needed for advertising and inventory. In retailing, Cary found, your best offense is your "sales or profit per square foot," which are measures of your department's productivity. There is a discrete amount of space on a store's floor, and each buyer fights for every available square foot. As a buyer in the home furnishings division, Cary also was responsible for decorative pillows, hassocks, and beanbag chairs.

One afternoon Cary found a business card on his desk with a note written on the back asking him, "How would you like to sell beanbags chairs for $19.99?" He was intrigued and contacted the salesperson. Once they spoke, a two-level negotiation began, first with Cary's merchandise manager and then with the beanbag chair sales representative.

The initial cost per beanbag chair was $10.00 plus freight with a target sale price at $19.99. The mark-up was less than the 50 percent requirement for that department. Cary's merchandise manager demanded that he maintain the department mark-up, so Cary had no choice but to go back and renegotiate the price with the sales representative. They settled on $9.50 per beanbag chair based on the purchase of a truckload. Cary, in fact, ordered three truckloads for the Memorial Day sale. He was very nervous; three truckloads equaled over one thousand beanbag chairs. He negotiated additional advertising money from his merchandise manager, and the store ran a half-page color ad in the Sunday *New York Daily News* featuring the beanbag chairs at $19.99.

The results were amazing. By Sunday night, they had sold every beanbag chair they had ordered, and on Tuesday morning, Cary was in his boss' office with purchase orders for three more truckloads to fill the orders still open. Because of this unexpected success, Cary no longer needed to ask for additional space or sales support; it was offered to him. What changed? He had both information power and economic power because he had successfully sold over two thousand beanbag chairs in one week. He also had referent power; Cary's boss was his biggest advocate as long as the chairs kept selling. The balance of that year the store sold over $600,000 in beanbag chairs. It was a one-time event, a fad, not a trend. The next year sales dropped dramatically as every one of Cary's competitors in New York City offered $19.99 beanbag chairs.

They say "success breeds success" and success certainly builds your prestige, reputation, and your level of knowledge as perceived by others. As a buyer, Cary suddenly had "expert power." In retailing, once you have success, you want to get promoted and let the next person deal with replicating your success. In the following year, Cary was not able to replicate those sales levels and lost some prestige in the organization. He no longer had any leverage in future negotiations with his merchandise manager.

Dealing with the Office Bully

In almost every office, there is an individual who is the "Office Bully." This bullying is manifested by a number of behaviors, including making outrageous demands, insisting that others agree to the position he takes, and threatening to walk away from any negotiation. Cary regularly participates in a number of online negotiation chat rooms. Recently he posted a question regarding bullying in the workplace. Immediately he received this response: "There is nothing more emotionally taxing in the world of negotiation than dealing with this type of personality!"

Another blogger observed that the bully is usually a coward on the inside. So knowing that little factoid can change your approach to the situation. Cary sees it as a "big tell," and it influences his preference in negotiating. In their 1991 book *Getting to Yes: Negotiating Agreement Without Giving In,* Roger Fisher and William Ury wrote about "going to the balcony." (This book was one of the basic texts Cary used in his graduate class on negotiation.) The phrase "going to the balcony" denotes you need to step out of the situation and see what is really happening in the negotiation from a different perspective. Once you recognize the tactics of the bully, you can respond with strength by saying, "Unless we can find a middle ground, we may not be successful in reaching an agreement."

When dealing with a bully, it all depends whether the negotiation is a one-time deal or whether you are trying to become strategic partners. Let's look at what Ury said about bullies in his second book *Getting Past No: Negotiating Your Way from Confrontation to Cooperation.* He wrote, "They need to know that the only way they can win is if they cooperate." His strategy of "building a golden bridge" requires both parties in a negotiation to work toward building a path to agreement.

Research shows that 70 percent of bullies are men. In his research, Cary discovered that there are four types of bullies: the cyber bully, the serial bully, the control freak, and the pressurized bully. Their goals range from just causing someone misery to amassing power.

The first bullying behavior, the cyber bully, was defined in the article "Bullying Definitions" by the nonprofit Respect (www.respect2all.org/bullying=definition/):

- Cyber bullies use information and communication technologies, such as Twitter, Facebook, and email, to support their deliberate, repeated, and hostile behavior that is intended to harm their target.

Serial bully, control freak, and pressurized bully were defined in the article "Types of Bullying" by the experts at Bullyonline.org, a

project of the Tim Field Foundation (http://bullyonline.org/index.php/
bullying/2-types-of-bullying):

- The serial bully is a person who mercilessly bullies one person after
  another, but whose depravity appears to be constrained by the
  understanding that he has to appear to behave decently to blend in with
  civilized people. Rather than using physical violence, he abuses people
  with methods that are harder for onlookers to notice, such as emotional
  blackmail and abusing the authority that comes with his job. The serial
  bully feels threatened by colleagues with competence, integrity, and
  popularity, and sooner or later he picks one out and projects onto him
  his own inadequacy and incompetence. Using unwarranted criticism
  and threats, he controls and subjugates his victim, without a thought
  for the contribution the coworker makes to the organization, or any
  concern for his victim's self-esteem, self-confidence, loyalty, or health.

- Control freaks tend to publicly admonish their inferiors, especially
  during meetings. There may be a fine line between being a detail-
  oriented manager who likes to have things done "right," and being a
  (destructive) control freak. In some cases, the control freak sees his
  constant intervention as beneficial or even necessary. Control freaks
  may so greatly enjoy the feeling of power that they automatically try to
  gain control of everything and everyone around them.

- The pressurized bully forces fellow employees to work within
  unrealistic time frames and/or with inadequate resources, causing a
  devaluation of personal life (particularly with salaried workers who are
  not compensated for their extra hours).

As an organizational behaviorist, Cary has a concern that people
involved in a negotiation try to label their counterpart's behavior as bullying or overly aggressive. He would rather see people deal directly with the
person's behavior. Cary has found that the best way to deal with a bully or
someone who is overly aggressive is to let the person know there are consequences to his behavior, including the possibility that he may lose the
opportunity to achieve a deal.

Here are some phrases you could use when dealing with bullying behaviors:

1. Call out the behavior in an observation and link it to a common goal. For example, "I think we both want to find a solution to this problem, but it is going to be difficult with you yelling" (or interrupting or shouting or name calling, etc.).

2. "I can see that you are feeling pretty upset" (frustrated, angry, etc.). That usually elicits an agreement and helps diffuse emotions.

3. "Do we need a break to give you some time?" (I try not to say the obvious: "to calm yourself down.")

4. "It is obvious that we are not going to make any progress today, so let's set another time to talk."

5. "I can't see how an agreement can be reached if this behavior continues."

One key tool to use is a *negative strip-line*. A strip-line tactic is a phrase or statement that signals the other negotiator that a change is needed in behavior in order to proceed to an agreement. The phrase in number five above is an example of a strip-line tactic. By using more negative statements to let him know that he might not accomplish his goal, you should see his emotions come slightly back to a more neutral state. If you don't see this happen, you either picked a poor statement or the other party is bluffing to obtain additional concessions.

A colleague of Cary's observed in an online blog, "Why waste valuable time arguing? Both people have responsibilities, and if nothing is being accomplished, why proceed? Aren't all negotiators good actors? We all play a role when negotiating, and it is dependent on with whom we are negotiating. In some cases, I end up educating the other negotiator as to how best to approach the problem. I usually get a positive response." It is all about being collaborative and building a relationship.

An option Cary has used to deal with a bully is to request changing the players in the negotiations. This strategy was used successfully in a past labor contract negotiation. He told the union regional vice president of UNITE (the combination of the ILGWU and ACWA) that he could not see making any progress with the union team currently in place. The VP came in from the New York office and took control of his team. The negotiation moved forward, and they reached an agreement.

Even more important, Cary strives to increase the amount of time, energy, money, and emotion the other party must spend to come to an agreement. Making a "bully" and his team work harder to get to an agreement is always beneficial. Typically, no matter how great they think they are at strong-arming, the more blood, sweat, and tears they spend, the harder it is for them to walk away from reaching an agreement.

Negotiating with Vendors

As you move up the corporate ladder, the types of negotiations you are involved in become more complex, and stressful, and they involve more players. Many times these complex negotiations reach an impasse and require the assistance of an outside party in order to restart the process.

Businesses depend on positive relationships with their suppliers. As a home furnishings buyer at Federated Department Stores, a major New York retailer, Cary negotiated pricing, delivery, merchandise returns, advertising support, and merchandising assistance. As the director of purchasing at the same retailer, he negotiated leasing agreements, production, and delivery schedules for critical supplies, as well as the recycling of corrugated boxes and the disposal of trash.

In some cases, there was an existing agreement that required adjustments only for the cost-of-living index. In other cases, new specifications had to be developed, and requests for a price quotation needed to be mailed to the approved vendors. Once bids were received, they had to be interpreted and compared against current pricing. Interpretation means recalculation of the bids so that they were "apples to apples" and a fair comparison.

Once Cary requested an annual bid on toilet paper, but misinterpreted the bids when they were received. He based his comparison on the case price instead of the cost per linear sheet of paper and mistakenly awarded the contract to a particular vendor. When he realized his error, he had to go back to the awarded vendor with "egg on his face" and retract the award. It was a very embarrassing situation—and the result of poor preparation.

How could Cary have been better prepared for this negotiation and avoided making an error that required him to have to save face?

1. He should have developed appropriate criteria on which to base his decision and requested the pricing be at the lowest common denominator, the price per linear sheet.

2. He should have garnered both information and expert power by speaking with other purchasing agents within Federated Department Stores about the best way to compare prices and by also asking them to review the Request for Price Quotation (RFQ).

Instead, he made a rookie mistake and almost incurred a significant increase in expense for the company. After that experience, Cary was more careful in developing bid requests and executing contracts.

Another potential pitfall in these types of negotiations include not clearly developing your RFQ, which should specify the following:

- Quantity
- Delivery frequency (weekly, monthly, or quarterly)
- Specifications as to assortments, quality, and labeling
- Design, color, packaging, and materials (such as gift boxes or corrugated boxes)

The more precise the specifications, the lower the possibility for error and the more accurate the pricing will be. As you negotiate, you must ask questions that allow you to gather the information you need to better execute your negotiation. Some suggested questions are:

- Where is the next volume price break?
- Will combining orders offer a price advantage?
- Would a small change in specifications result in a price change (many times products are over-specified)?
- Would committing to a longer contract length lower the price of the service or product?

These questions and others will result in better pricing, service levels, and relationships with your suppliers. Always have one or more back-up vendors, as these become your BATNAs in case your negotiations break down or you cannot achieve your price and delivery goals with your existing vendor. Having one or more back-up suppliers strengthens your position and permits you to walk away from a poor deal.

Understand that vendors also make honest mistakes when they reply to an RFQ. The question is, "How will you react when you realize they made an error in their bid?" This happened to Cary, and he contacted the vendor and advised him that his quoted price was more than 10 percent lower than his bid in the previous year. Cary inquired as to what changes the vendor had made to his process that permitted him to reduce his costs. The vendor responded that he had changed nothing and requested that he be given time to review the bid. After a day he responded that his estimator had left out the profit margin from the bid. He resubmitted a revised bid and was awarded a portion of the annual contract. He also stated that he was very embarrassed and appreciated that Cary permitted him to review his initial bid and resubmit a corrected bid.

Cary could have held him to the lower price, but the vendor would have never shipped the product and that action could have damaged their mutual business relationship and Cary's reputation in the market. Because Cary gave him a chance to "save face," the vendor now owed Cary a "chip" to be played at another time. The manner in which Cary handled this transaction resulted in the strengthening of their business relationship and increasing their respect for each other. On the contrary, because of the size of national retailers such as Amazon, Macy's, and Sam's Club, it is not unusual these days to see buyers leveraging their "economic power" and taking advantage of vendors. Since the relationships between buyers and vendors tend to be one-sided anyway, the result could be destructive to a business relationship.

Negotiating with Customers

As a business owner or a manger, you need to negotiate with your customers to solve problems, secure orders, and maintain a mutually beneficial relationship. Here are some suggestions:

1. *Solving problems.* When you own or run a business, you will always be challenged to solve problems. This is a normal part of conducting business.

   a. Your first step is to acknowledge that there is a problem. Delaying or ignoring a problem only makes it worse, as the solution will be more expensive to implement, and the relationship with the customer will likely will be damaged.

   b. Your next step is to ask the customer to clearly define the problem and identify potential solutions. Don't offer a solution until you totally understand the details of the problem. The best solution may not be the first one that comes to mind.

   c. Once you have clearly defined the problem and developed your proposed solutions, you need to evaluate the customer's suggested solutions and compare them to the solutions you have developed.

d. Whatever solution you select, it should be a "win-win" for both sides. In some cases, you may have to give up something in the short term in order to retain the customer.

e. If the problem was actually caused by the customer, link your solution to a change in their business behavior. Linking is tying a change in behavior or a concession the customer makes to a concession you may make. You should never make a concession unless the customer also gives up something of value. This provides for a truly collaborative approach to problem solving.

2. *Securing orders.* Many times when you are negotiating a deal, the buyer may state "the price is too high" or "I need the delivery by a certain date."

a. When you hear that the price is "too high," you have a number of options available: you can reduce your price by a set percentage, ask "What part of the price is too high," or suggest they move to the next price break point.

Determining *exactly* which component of the price is too high helps to identify the best solution to the price problem. It may be the freight, the size of the discount, or the unit cost. All it may take is a small adjustment to the quantity or the unit cost to seal the deal. Offering a percentage off, 10 percent for example, may give away too much of your margin.

b. The request of "delivery by a certain date" is another opportunity to manage a potential problem. Cary has run into this problem and found that asking, "Do you need the entire quantity on that date?" revealed that the answer was often "no." That opened up the opportunity to ask a *follow-up* question. "How much do you need by that delivery date?" You may find out that you can fulfill the entire order over a set period of time, avoid additional costs, and keep the customer satisfied.

Both of these situations offer you the opportunity to identify options with your customer by maintaining an ongoing dialogue. This type of dialogue will strengthen the relationship between the parties and create a win-win situation. Your vendors and customers will become your business partners, because together you are solving problems in a manner that benefits all parties.

Resolving a Dispute

Should the parties to any of the following business negotiation scenarios reach an impasse, there are options. Many purchase orders and contracts contain a clause that permits the parties to introduce a third party into the negotiation when an impasse is reached. Many contracts stipulate ADR (Alternative Dispute Resolution), which involves mediation and, in some cases, arbitration. If the parties cannot reach an agreement within a reasonable period of time, ADR will be implemented. The process of mediation usually results in a win-win agreement, while arbitration awards tend to be a zero-sum result, in which one party is made whole at the expense of the other party. This result does not aid in maintaining a positive long-term relationship.

Negotiating in a Family Business

Family-owned businesses operate differently from traditional enterprises. In many cases, there are no organizational charts, and roles are not clearly defined. In addition, the locus of power resides with the family members. If you are part of—or working in—a family-owned business, it would not be unusual to find yourself in the middle of a disagreement among family members.

Negotiating within the family setting is totally different from other business negotiations. Relationships among most of the players are long standing, and it is likely that they have strong emotional ties to each other. Parents negotiating with their sons and daughters as well as siblings negotiating with each other, offer challenges not present in most other business-related negotiation scenarios. Just because the people in the business share the same last name, it does not preclude conflict over how they define the business and its markets.

Research performed by Davis and Malhotra at Harvard University in 2007 shows that family members in business together have trouble listening without judging each other—more so than business partners who are unrelated. They stated that the best family-based negotiations are ones that involve multiple interests. Negotiating the dual standards of "what is good for the family" and "what is good for the business" is a serious challenge, as sometimes these standards are in opposition to each other.

Finding common ground in a family business. In a family-owned business, family members usually prefer to reach solutions that are mutually acceptable. A March 2012 article on the IMD website titled "Negotiating in the Family Business" by Professors Suzanne de Janasz and Joachim Schwass discussed the challenges involved in finding common ground. The assumption that sharing the same name means that you have to share the same views may lead family members to self-censor and prevent them from suggesting an outside-the-box solution. Such a solution would be one that does not follow the current philosophy or direction of the business. When one or more family members proposes a new way of conducting business, they are concerned that they could face strong opposition from other family members who might quickly respond, "This is not the way we conduct our business." Both communication and candor need to increase to end this kind of potential impasse. To be successful, a negotiated solution would need to meet the criterion of what is best for both the business and the owners.

Cary served as a senior vice president of a fifty-year-old, family-owned apparel business where he was exposed to generational interactions and conflicts. It was the owner's desire that his three children would have roles in the future of the business. Other members of the extended family were also involved in various aspects of the company. This made any negotiation a multilevel one, and more complex.

As a non-family member, Cary found it difficult to negotiate changes that were necessary to improve the conduct and profitability of the business. Many times he was met with the statement, "It's my business," which immediately extinguished Cary's request for the suggested changes. The owner was a "micro-manager" and a "control taker" who desired to put his personal stamp on all major decisions, which slowed the process down. There was no formal decision-making process. The business had grown rapidly and needed to be professionally managed in order to continue in the growth mode.

What Cary found effective was to translate his proposed changes into financially based decisions and use information power. What his boss did understand was how these decisions impacted the company's bottom line, its profitability. This provided Cary the leverage he needed to convince his boss that the proposed changes were in his best interests as the owner and best for his company. By striving to create more value for the company, and discussing the impact on profitability, Cary created common ground with his boss, who then was open to accept the requested changes.

Power relationships. Power is a major component in any business negotiation, but even more so when family members are involved. In a family-owned business, the succeeding generations are not only dealing with their boss but also with their father, mother, or even an older sibling. The older members can leverage information power, expert power, and legitimate power when negotiating with the younger generations. The founding generation and siblings may also use a negative power source, coercive power. Examples of coercive power include bullying or threatening to terminate an employee. They may state, "Unless I get your cooperation in this situation, I will involve my father." This is coercive because of the implied threat.

The younger generation, because of its education levels, may also be able to use information power on a limited basis in a negotiation. Additionally, the younger generation can align themselves with one or more member of the founding generation and establish a high degree of associative power to be used in a negotiation with another family member.

Outside influences. Jealousy can impact the relationship between siblings and their significant others, wives, or husbands. These distractions and potential conflicts can be eliminated by keeping the non-stockholders (spouses and significant others) out of the business decision-making process. This is where the adage "ignorance is bliss" applies. It is best not to have spouses involved unless they possess expertise that would improve the performance of the business.

It is critical in these family business negotiation situations that outside influences, such as friends of the owners and their business associates, are also kept out of the discussions. Developing and agreeing on an agenda for the negotiation, in which the specific topics and speakers for each topic are delineated, will help to prevent others from inappropriately being involved. Agendas help the parties focus on the issues at hand and allocate time to discuss these agreed-upon issues. Each of the family members can submit items for the agenda. Critical information must be disseminated to all the parties involved prior to the negotiation.

Succession planning. It is very important that a family-owned and operated company has a clear plan of succession to ensure that when there is a transition in leadership, the person who takes over the company is suitably prepared. Not having a succession plan can significantly impact the success and even the continued existence of a company, especially if the company's owner were to pass away unexpectedly. Cary has worked with several companies that did not have a formal succession plan, which eventually led to the dissolution or sale of the business.

Creating a succession plan is more than just deciding who will assume the leadership of the company at the time of a transition. It involves careful thought and planning, as the decision of who will run the business in the future should be based on business acumen and management capabilities, not birth order. The "heir(s) apparent" (most often the children) need to be properly groomed to ensure that they have the necessary knowledge, skills, and experience to assume their future roles in the organization. Ideally they would be mentored not only by the head of the company but by non-family members as well in learning the ins and outs of the business.

In some cases, one sibling will learn faster than the others. There also may be differences in siblings' levels of motivation and interpersonal skills. Often the second generation will mimic the management style of their parents, especially if the parents have been successful.

To prepare for a successful transition in leadership, the parent should move his children and other family members up the corporate ladder as they demonstrate that they have mastered the skills necessary to learn, motivate, train, and lead. The parent must be inclusive, and must emphasize that his children (or relatives) need to *earn* their places in the organization. When children and relatives of the owner move up the ladder without the necessary skills or accomplishments, company morale at all levels—management team, frontline supervisors, and even line staff—will suffer.

Sometimes the vision parents have for the business could be very different from the one that their children have and could be a potential source of generational conflict. Cary has heard many business owners say, "I am building this business for my children." This statement is not always accurate, however. In many situations, the children have ambitions other than running the family business. Many of the business leaders of the Millennial Generation would rather plot their own path to success or may not be as passionate as their parents about investing the necessary "sweat equity" to continue the family business. On the other hand, Millennials who were raised in the family business and have the entrepreneurial drive of their parent will most likely gladly invest the time to learn every aspect of the business and eventually to run it.

Cary was brought into one business to help resolve a conflict between siblings because the father desired to turn over the business he had built to two of his sons. They asked Cary to determine what could be done to reduce the level of conflict between the two siblings as they had a history of disagreements that dated back to their childhood. In fact, the two brothers had already forced a third brother out of the business.

After repeated efforts to mediate their disputes and differences in management styles, Cary had no choice but to suggest that the father choose one of two alternatives: sell the business to a third party and divide the assets among the family members, or split the business along geographic lines and provide each son with his own entity. Ultimately the father chose the second option and provided each son the opportunity to run his own business without the need for the two of them to interact regularly with each other. This solution provided a "win" for all the involved parties: the owner, the two brothers, and their employees.

A client of Cary's who had two sons working in his construction business is another example of a father/owner who anticipated his retirement and who planned ahead for it. He was determined that the best way to continue the growth of the company after his exit was to split the business into two separate entities that would support each son's growth. Ultimately the business was divided into a construction entity and a development entity, with each brother heading up one company. They collaborated on projects, but each brother had his own business to run and develop.

The difference between the two examples is that one decision was reactive and the other was proactive. Thinking through and planning for change increases the likelihood of a successful transition and reduces the potential for conflict among the family members, especially when they are involved in the decision-making process.

The whole process of grooming family members to take over a family business can be full of conflict and requires open communication throughout. In many companies, the founders had a vision, followed it, and watched their business grow. When the business owner's sons or daughters return to the business after completing an MBA or law or accounting degree, plus having acquired valuable real-life experiences, they may have a different vision for the company. It is important that the founding member of the business be open to these ideas and at least be willing to listen to their children's ideas and reasons for making these recommendations.

If one or more of the siblings does not have an interest in being involved in the family business, how do the other children resolve this potential conflict? There is no guarantee that the next generation will have an interest in being involved in the business or have the skills needed to run it. If that is the case, the founder of the business needs to plan ahead to develop an exit strategy that ideally would enable the family to protect their employees as well as the family's income stream.

Lessons Learned

- When applying for a position, prepare an updated resume and customize your cover letter for the desired position, using the job description as your focus. For each resume you are submitting, match your skills to those outlined in the job description.

- Be prepared to present a counter offer in a "neutral" manner. For example, you may say, "Based on my budget I require this level of salary to be able to live in your location." You have the option to be more direct and confident when you have an offer from another firm (your **BATNA** or **B**est **A**lternative **T**o a **N**egotiated **A**greement). If the company really wants you, they will attempt to match or exceed the other offer. You need to consider what you will do if they say "no" to your counter offer. Never offer an ultimatum unless you are prepared to carry it out.

- By participating in previous interviews, you gain valuable experience. You will better understand the process and the salary ranges and benefits, and you will have built your self-confidence, which sets you apart from other potential candidates.

- Performance appraisals are a collaborative conversation between individuals about opportunities to increase an individual's skill sets and value to the employer. The keys to a successful performance appraisal lie in detailed preparation and the ability of both parties to communicate the importance of maintaining or improving an individual's performance.

- It is important to identify common ground with your negotiation counterpart. These parallel interests can serve as a "jumping off point" for your negotiation. This information will also help you to begin to build a foundation for current and future solutions that will best meet the needs of both parties.

- To be successful in business, it is important to be aware of and learn how to work with—or at least adapt to—the leadership style of your superior. Does your supervisor tend to be more autocratic or more inclusive? Being aware of your boss's leadership style will provide guidance in figuring out the best way to negotiate with him.

(continued)

- The management style demonstrated by the founder of the business can greatly impact whether the company will grow or fail. The dictator will be the locus of power and decision-making, often strangling the business. The inclusive leader involves subordinates and employees in the decisions that determine the direction and growth of the business.

- Every office has its "bully." The best way to deal with a bully is to let him know there are consequences to his behavior, including the possibility that he may lose the opportunity to achieve his goals if the behavior continues. Let him know how you feel and that you will not be his target.

- Businesses depend on positive relationships with both customers and vendors. Your vendors and customers will become your business partners when you negotiate with them in a collaborative manner and seek mutually acceptable solutions to problems. Collaborative "win-win" negotiations build trust and long-term relationships.

- Family-owned businesses operate differently from traditional enterprises. In many cases, there are no organizational charts, and roles are not clearly defined. In addition, the locus of power resides with the family members. It is not unusual to find yourself in the middle of a disagreement among family members.

- Finding common ground with your negotiating counterpart in a family business can sometimes be challenging, but it is important if you are going to develop a creative solution that satisfies the needs of both parties.

- To be successful, a negotiated solution would meet the criterion of "what is best for both the business and its owners."

- It is not unusual for one sibling to align himself with one or more of the older family members and in that manner practice "associative power"—the power of whom you know or associate with. He would then attempt to use the other person's position as leverage in the negotiation.

- During negotiations in a family business, it is critical that non-stockholders, including spouses and friends, are not part of the negotiating process.

- A family-owned and operated company needs to have a clear plan of succession to ensure that when there is a transition in leadership, the person who takes over the company is suitably prepared. Not having a succession plan can significantly impact the success and even the continued existence of a company, especially if the company's owner were to pass away unexpectedly.

CHAPTER TWELVE

The Last Word

As Samantha, Jerry, Dan, and Jon continue on their journeys, they will add the necessary negotiating and communication tools to their toolbox. They will find a level of comfort in their approach to any negotiating situation and be able to defuse the potential conflicts, use the appropriate power for the situation, and develop options during their planning process. By incorporating these behaviors into their daily activities and interactions, they will overcome their negotiaphobia and achieve a high level of success.

A s you mature from adolescent to adult to parent and grandparent, your negotiation journey will continue. While on this journey, you will gain experience, hone your communication skills, and become more comfortable entering into and conducting complex, multi-issue negotiations. Preparation is the road that leads to success in any negotiation; preparation results in less time required for executing and monitoring your agreement.

Critical to success in any complex negotiation is completing the alphabet game. You need to know your BATNA, WATNA, and ZOPA. (These alphabet tools are defined both in Chapter Two and in the Glossary of Terms.) By completing these tools, you identify the range of acceptable and unacceptable outcomes and alternatives to suggested agreements. Knowing these tools provides you with an edge in your negotiation.

Both of us have stressed that ground rules are very important to conducting any negotiation and need to be articulated early on in the negotiation process. An agenda aids you in formalizing the negotiation and identifies the items that are going to be discussed. In a business negotiation, both sides should exchange agendas and agree upon what will be discussed during the initial meeting. This is the first stage of the negotiation: the parties discuss and agree what will be on the agenda and where and when to meet.

We have addressed the many sensitive topics that need to be negotiated with your spouse, children, and parents. The phrase "timing is everything" comes to mind when thinking about these sensitive topics. The earlier you negotiate topics such as the surrendering of the car keys and final arrangements, the better the chance you will succeed. Knowing that you will meet resistance, you need to plant the seed as early as possible. In order to be successful in these sensitive areas, you need to line up support with your siblings and other influencers prior to beginning the negotiation process. Their agreement with your approach and strategies will be critical to providing the support you need to prevail.

Just as older adults cherish their independence and privacy, adolescents desire to be in control and resist imposed rules when it comes to driving, chores, curfew, and dating. Negotiations with adolescents need to be handled with "kid gloves" and with a great deal of sensitivity to the teen's feelings and beliefs. Trust needs to be built between the parties. You must emphasize that you are concerned with their safety and that they are loved, which are your primary motivations.

During any negotiation there are potential "pitfalls" or "hot buttons" that need to be recognized and avoided. In a number of chapters, we have provided examples of these challenges and also how to identify and deal with your hot buttons and those of your negotiating partner. Any negotia-tor needs to understand his or her opposition and how the opposition tends to approach and execute a negotiation. That is why each of us needs to take into account gender and culture when preparing for a negotiation.

Again, in a business negotiation scenario, the key is preparation. Use Google, Dogpile, or some other search engine to gather information about your negotiation counterpart. You may be able to gather information on how she approaches a negotiation, her ethics, and her reputation. This information could provide valuable insights into her behavior in a negotia-tion. You will also find it helpful to contact others who have dealt with these individuals in business and collect their insights.

As you continue your life's journey, you will build confidence in your abilities, learn to trust your new skills, and find that each negotiation is unique and requires an investment of your time to be successful. Now you have acquired the insights and skills to reduce or extinguish your negotia-phobia. We wish you good luck and success in all your current and future negotiations.

About the Authors

Larry Waldman, PhD, ABPP, has been a clinical forensic psychologist in private practice in Phoenix, Arizona, for nearly forty years. Larry earned his BS in Education and Psychology from the University of Wisconsin-Madison, his MS in School Psychology from the University of Wisconsin-Milwaukee, and his PhD in Educational Psychology from Arizona State University. He acquired his ABPP

(Certified member of American Board of Professional Psychology) in 2003.

Overcoming Your NegotiaPhobia is Dr. Waldman's sixth book. His other books are: *Who's Raising Whom? A Parent's Guide to Effective Child Discipline, Coping with Your Adolescent, How Come I Love Him but Can't Live with Him? The Graduate Course You Never Had: How To Develop, Manage and Market a Flourishing Mental Health Practice,* and *Too Busy Earning a Living to Make Your Fortune? Discover the Psychology of Achieving Your Life Goals.*

Larry's articles have been published in both the local and national press. He consults with the Social Security Administration office in Phoenix and with family law attorneys, and is an adjunct graduate professor at Northern Arizona University. He speaks nationally to fellow mental health providers, attorneys, chiropractors, corporations, and the public on marriage, parenting, private practice development, stress management, psychotherapy, wellness, and Post Traumatic Stress Disorder (PTSD).

Larry and his wife Nan reside in Scottsdale, Arizona, but spend the summer in Southern California. They have two sons: Joshua, a litigation attorney who is married to Natalie, a speech and language pathologist. They have a young son, which makes Larry a "Papa." Chad is a school psychologist and is married to Emily, an urban planner.

Cary Silverstein, MBA, has extensive experience in business, vendor, and labor negotiations. He earned his BA in Political Science and Industrial Psychology from CUNY's Queens College. His MBAs in Marketing and Organizational Behavior were awarded by The Arthur B. Roth School of Business at Long Island University. He attended Marquette University in Milwaukee and was awarded a Certificate in Labor Management Rela-

tions. Cary has also attended advanced negotiation training at Harvard's Program on Negotiation (PON).

As president of his consulting firm, SMA, LLC, Cary has mentored and trained middle- and upper-level executives at Fortune 500 companies in the art and science of negotiation. He has authored over 130 articles for *The BizTimes Milwaukee* and has published articles in a number of other national business periodicals as well as in England, Australia, and on the Internet. He served as a senior adjunct professor at two Midwest universities for over thirty years, and lectured on negotiation theory and strategy to hundreds of graduate students. Cary was also a vice president of LERA (Labor Employment Relations Association) and represented the management side of labor relations. He is a former president of the Milwaukee North Shore Rotary Club and a recipient of the Paul Harris Award.

Cary and his wife Susie live in Milwaukee, Wisconsin, but spend the winter months in Scottsdale, Arizona. Cary and Susie have two children. Son Bradley is a senior flight test engineer at Cessna. Bradley and his wife Cindy, who live in Kansas, are the parents of Cary and Susie's four grandchildren and the grandparents of Cary and Susie's great-granddaughter. Cary and Susie's daughter Lesley, an artist and screenwriter, lives in Westwood, California.

Glossary of Terms

Active listening is a communication technique that permits the negotiator to validate and clarify the statements being made by the other negotiator. This technique reduces the potential for misunderstandings by the use of probing and paraphrasing techniques.

An *agenda* is a list of the topics to be discussed/negotiated by the parties. It also specifies the location and time of the negotiation. Each of the parties should be asked to provide topics for the discussion/ negotiation. The agenda should be sent out in advance. This is the first step in the negotiation process and permits the parties to begin to build trust.

Alternative Dispute Resolution (ADR) is a process that permits the parties to break an impasse with the assistance of a third party. The third party could be a mediator, arbitrator, or facilitator. Mediators assist the parties to craft their own resolution. An arbitrator hears evidence and then rules for one of the parties. A facilitator also helps the parties to a resolution.

Anchoring is the technique of initiating a conversation with a positive statement in order to gain and maintain the other person's attention. As a result, the person will be more open to what is being said. An example of an anchoring statement is: "I feel that working together we can develop a solution that will benefit both parties."

Associative power is derived from whom you know or are associated with, both inside or outside an organization. An example is when a father and a son in a family business form an alliance to fight off an initiative from another family member in the business. By aligning with a major stockholder of the company, the father and son would gain additional associative power over the other family member.

BATNA is your **B**est **A**lternative **T**o a **N**egotiated **A**greement. Don't enter into any negotiation without having one or more alternative agreements in mind. Having an actionable BATNA provides you with the power to walk away. Having negotiated a BATNA gives the negotiator insight into the true bargaining range from the information gathered during the development of each alternative.

Boomerang Generation is the generation of young adults, eighteen to thirty-five, in the Western culture who have moved back into their parents' home after college or graduate school because they are not financially independent.

Coercive power is destructive and is derived from using negative behaviors such as threats and bullying, or from a person's position in a family, organization, or business. Using coercive power could have a negative impact on long-term relationships.

Collaborative means demonstrating a high degree of concern for the substance of the negotiation, the issues being discussed, and the relationship between the parties. This behavior is characterized by searching creatively for common interests with the other party. A collaborative negotiator demonstrates problem-solving behavior and builds synergistic solutions that work for both parties by linking the solutions to the issues being discussed.

Collaborative divorce is a type of divorce in which each party is supported by a team of experts as they negotiate the divorce in a non-litigious setting.

Common ground refers to areas of agreement between the parties in a negotiation. It is helpful to try to identify these areas prior to beginning a negotiation, as they will provide a positive "jumping off" point from which to begin.

Cross-cultural negotiations are complicated negotiations that occur between individuals from two different cultures and backgrounds. Negotiators involved in these situations should seek assistance from consultants who are experienced in these countries and are familiar with their cultural norms.

Cueing is an indirect suggestion, hint, or secondary stimulus that guides behavior, often without entering the person's consciousness. Cueing can also be a signal or reminder to do something. In psychology, it is the part of any sensory pattern that is identified as the signal for a response.

Downside risk is a term that describes the level of risk that exists or a potential penalty if an agreement is not reached by the parties. An example would be the dissolution of the relationship or a lost business opportunity.

Economic power is having the ability to influence a decision by threatening to withhold funds or labor. In labor management negotiations, for example, it is not uncommon for a union to threaten to withhold its workers by calling a strike in order to gain leverage in the negotiation of a contract.

Expert power is a subset of information power and a powerful tool to persuade your opponent that your data should form the basis of the agreement. Whenever possible, you should consult with experts to get their support of the position you are taking.

Gravity issue is a term used to describe a situation or condition that will not change and cannot be influenced. For example, if a union is representing your employees in a labor negotiation, there is no flexibility in regard to when the next contract is to be negotiated; under established federal law, you must negotiate a new contract when the current one expires.

Ground rules are rules designed to establish behavioral boundaries for the conduct of a negotiation. They include rules against the use of bluffing, lying, threats, and other unethical tactics in the negotiation process.

An *impasse* is reached when neither party can move past disagreement on a particular element in a negotiation. Impasses can be broken through the use of a neutral intermediary (mediation or arbitration) or by the parties themselves using collaborative negotiation techniques.

Information power is acquired by having the necessary data to support your position in a negotiation. It is the most powerful and effective tool you can have.

Legitimate power is based on an individual's position in an organization. Individuals who hold "C"-level positions (CEO, CFO, CIO, and COO) in a business have legitimate power simply by nature of their titles. Judges and other elected officials are other examples of people vested with legitimate power. Birth order is another source of legitimate power in a family setting.

A *mediator* is a neutral individual who works with all parties in order to craft a mutually acceptable solution to a problem. Mediators are used when an impasse is reached in business, labor, or divorce negotiations.

The Millennial Generation is the demographic cohort following Generation X. There is no precise age span for identifying Millennials; researchers and commentators use birth years ranging from the early 1980s to the early 2000s. In 2014, Paul Taylor and others from the Pew Research Center issued a report titled "Millennials in Adulthood: Detached from Institutions, Networked with Friends." The report said that Millennials are somewhat more upbeat than older adults about America's future, with 49 percent saying the country's best years are ahead, although they are the first generation in the modern era to have higher levels of student loan debt and unemployment than any prior generation.

Negotiaphobia is the fear and anxiety associated with negotiating over anything with anybody. It is associated with procrastination and the desire to preserve relationships even when they are flawed. It can be extinguished through preparation, practice, and success in a negotiation.

Prenup (prenuptial or premarital agreement, commonly shortened to prenup) is a contract entered into prior to marriage or civil union or any other prior agreement by people intending to marry or contract with each other. The content of a prenuptial agreement can vary widely but commonly includes provisions for division of property and spousal support in the event of death, divorce, or break-up of the marriage. It may also include further conditions of guardianship or terms for the forfeiture of assets as a result of divorce on the grounds of adultery.

Saving face is an ancient Asian tradition in which one person permits another to correct a mistake rather than taking advantage of the error. It is designed to build a relationship rather than destroy it.

Strip-line tactic is a phrase or statement that signals the other negotiator that a change is needed in behavior in order to proceed to an agreement. This tactic is especially effective when dealing with a "bully" negotiator.

Situational cue is something happening in our environment that we interpret as needing a response. Possible emotional responses to such a cue are: anger, fear, anxiety, and curiosity.

The *two-column approach* helps a negotiator identify the interests that both parties in a negotiation have in common. Either negotiator would list the interests of each party on a single sheet of paper and then find "common interests" from which to launch the negotiation. This is the first step toward a collaborative outcome.

WATNA is the **W**orst **A**lternative **T**o a **N**egotiated **A**greement. You need to know where the line in the sand is drawn when you are negotiating. Without an identified WATNA, you could end up agreeing to a deal that does not satisfy your basic interests. Your WATNA is the lower end of your bargaining range and should be identified prior to starting the negotiation

A *zero sum game* is like playing a poker hand in which one party wins and one party loses. There is no mutual gain. This type of result does not build trust or a relationship. In many cases, it builds resentment and could lead to retaliatory behavior when the parties next negotiate.

By developing your **ZOPA** (**Z**one of **P**otential **A**greement), you identify three possible options in the zone: *Aspire to* is the level of agreement at which you get the maximum, the win. *Content with* provides both sides with a win. Usually a collaborative agreement is the result. *Live with* is a deal that gets you the minimum you desire.

Bibliography

Blanchard, Ken, and Spencer Johnson. *The One Minute Manager.* New York: Berkley Trade, 1982.

Davidds, Yasmin, with Ann Bidou. *On Your Own Terms: A Women's Guide to Taking Charge of Any Negotiation.* New York: AMACOM, 2015.

Davis, John A., and Deepak Malhotra. "Five Steps to Better Family Negotiations." *Harvard Business Review* (July 2006).

Fisher, Roger, and William Ury. *Getting to Yes,* 2nd ed. New York: Penguin Books, 1991.

Glaser, Connie, and Barbara Steinberg Smalley. *Swim With the Dolphins: How Women Can Succeed in Corporate America on Their Own Terms.* New York: Warner Books, 1995.

Herman, Gregg. "The Ultimatum Game and Divorce Negotiations." *American Journal of Law,* no. 27, vol. 2 (Summer 2013).

Pradel, Dina W., Hannah Riley Bowles, and Kathleen L. McGinn. "When Gender Changes the Negotiation." Harvard Business School newsletter *Working Knowledge* (February 2006).

Silverstein, Cary. "Are You a Pawn Star?" *BizTimes Milwaukee* (April 5, 2013).

Silverstein, Cary. "The Gender Guard," *Small Business Times,* Milwaukee (September 18, 2008).

Silverstein, Cary. "Gender Mender." *Small Business Times,* Milwaukee (October 17, 2008).

"Ten Commandments of Good Behavior." New York: American Management Association (1961).

Ury, William. *Getting Past No: Negotiating Your Way From Confrontation to Cooperation.* New York: Bantam Books, 1993.

Waldman, Larry. *Who's Raising Whom? A Parent's Guide to Effective Child Discipline,* 4th ed. Phoenix: UCS Press, 2007.

Waldman, Larry. *Coping with Your Adolescent.* Norfolk, VA: Hampton Roads, 1994.

Waldman, Larry. *How Come I Love Him But Can't Live with Him? How to Make Your Marriage Work Better.* Milwaukee: Minuteman Press, 2002.

Webliography

"Age and Driving Safety Tips and Warning Signs for Older Drivers." www.helpguide.org/articles/aging-well/age-and-driving-safety-tips.htm

Barker, Eric. "How To Make Difficult Conversations Easy: Seven Steps From a Clinical Psychologist." www.bakadesuyo.com/2014/12/difficult-conversations/

Beckwith, Sandra. "How Can Men and Women Communicate Better with Each Other?" 2000. www.sandrabeckwith.com/articles/m-w-communicate.htm

Bullyonline. "Types of Bullying." January 15, 2006. www.bullyonline.org/index.php/bullying/2-types-of-bullying

Campbell, Rishona. "10 Pitfalls About Interracial Relationships." www.rishona.net/2011/12/27/10-pitfalls-about-interracial-relationships/

Collaborative Family Law Council of Wisconsin. www.collabdivorce.com

de Janasz, Suzanne, and Joachim Schwass. "Negotiating in the Family Business." IMD, March 2012. http://www.imd.org/research/challenges/negociation-family-business-conflict-suzanne-de-janasz-joachim-schwass.cfm

Gedeon, Kimberly. "All About The Swirl, Baby! Interracial Couples In The United States...By The Numbers." www.madamenoire.com/432922/swirl-interracial-couples-america-numbers/

Grind, Kirsten. "Mother, Can You Spare a Room?" www.wsj.com/'articles/SB10001424127887323699704578326583020869940

Grose, Jessica. "Married Interfaith Couples Who Keep Religious Traditions Separate on the Rise." www.slate.com/blogs/xx_factor/2014/interfaith_marriage_study_couples_who_keep_their_religious_traditions_separate.html

Hatfield, Heather. "How to handle toxic friends." WEBMD, January 26, 2006. www.cbsnews.com/news/how-to-handle-toxic-friends/

"Interracial Marriages in the US: Facts and Figures." *The New Observer*, TNO Staff, April 20, 2013. http://newobserveronline.com/interracial-marriages-in-the-us-facts-and-figures

Israel, Laurie. "5 Realities About Prenuptial Agreements—Why Having One May Be a Bad Choice For Your Marriage." www.ivkdlaw.com/the-firm/our-articles/prenuptial-agreements-and-lawyering/5-real

Itzhaki, Yael. "Negotiating through the Glass Ceiling." *EurekAlert*, American Friends of Tel Aviv University, June 25, 2008. https://www.eurekalert.org/pub_releases/2008-06/afot-ntt062508.php

Quesnel, Dawn. "What Are Your Hot Buttons? Issues, people, or situations that get under your skin!" http://coachdq.com/2011/07/9

Respect2all. "Bullying Definitions." http://respect2all.org/bullying-definitions/

Riley, Naomi Schaefer. "Interfaith Unions: A Mixed Blessing." www.nytimes.com/2013/04/06/opinion

Spero, Rand. "Adult Children Moving Back Home: The Boomerang Generation and the New Normal." www.mghclaycenter.org/parenting-concerns/young-adults/adult-children-moving-back-home-the boomerang-generation-new-normal/

Supgul, Alexander. "5 Warning Signs of a Toxic Friendship & Steps to Ending One." www.myfoxhouston.com/story/25823652/5-warning-signs-of-a-toxic-friendship-5-steps-to-ending-one

Taylor, Paul, Kim Parker, and Rich Morin. "Millennials in Adulthood: Detached from Institutions, Networked with Friends." Pew Research Center, March 7, 2014. http://www.pewsocialtrends.org/files/2014/03/2014-03-07_generations-report-version-for-web.pdf

Waldman, Larry. "Achieving 'OK' is 'Great' in Marriage." 2014. www.findapsychologist.org

"Who Can and Cannot be Included in Prenuptial Agreements." www.Findlaw.com/marriage/What-can-and-cannot-be-included-in-a-prenuptial-agreement-html

CPSIA information can be obtained
at www.ICGtesting.com
Printed in the USA
LVHW031512240919
632125LV00011B/1120/P